"The perfect companion for r
their baby."
Dr Carolyn Goh, BEng., MSc., PhD., MBBS, Author of *Baby
Bowen, Stop Wheezing Start Breathing* & *Bowen for Pregnancy and
Labour*

"The most recent, outstanding and updated natural and
macrobiotic baby book you must read! The definitive support
to secure health for your baby from the start."
Marijke De Coninck, Author of *Pure & Vegetarian*, Macrobiotic
Teacher & Counselor

"Charming and practical. Takes the mystery out of cooking
pure food. Babies are conscious from conception, their brains
are patterned by their environment, and this includes the food
we eat."
Kitty Hagenbach, co-founder of Babies Know with Dr Yehudi
Gordon

"Reassuring and supportive and full of good, healthy advice.
Highly recommended."
Michael Rossoff, L.Ac. Acupuncturist, Macrobiotic Teacher &
Counselor

"A wonderful reminder of the moment to moment wonder that
a new baby is. The foods are delicious and very beneficial. I
will recommend *Pure Baby* to all my expectant mothers."
Ana Maria Lavin, MBAC., MRCHM., DipAc., LicCHM.
Acupuncturist

"Valuable insights and gentle suggestions for mothers who are passionate about wholesome produce."
Kate Shepherd, Midwife, National Childbirth Trust & Bump & Baby Club Teacher

"A truly fantastic insight into giving your baby the healthiest and brightest start in life. Full of wonderful ideas and tips to aid your little ones' development and provide healthy and wholesome nutrition for you and baby."
Karen Luna, Baby Sensory teacher

"*Pure Baby* embodies much wisdom and practical knowledge."
Karen Mander, Hypnobirthing & Hypnofertility practitioner

"I have been inspired by the recipes and ideas for nourishing little ones and found the cookbook really useful, which I will return to often. So many mothers would benefit from the knowledge here!"
Rachel Lex, Midwife

"I'll be trying out the recipes and am inspired to cook healthier meals."
Grace Sabri, Sing And Sign Teacher

"I love *Pure Baby*. I felt with you as you journeyed through the first year. I wish *Pure Baby* had existed when I had my first baby and wanted ideas about a milk other than my own and a practical healthy route to weaning."
Helen Biscoe-Taylor, Psychotherapist and Parenting Coach

PURE BABY

GIVE A BEAUTIFUL BEGINNING

ANNA FREEDMAN

Published by Shambhala House, 77 Beak Street, London, W1F 9DB.

A CIP catalogue record for this book is available from the British Library.

ISBN 978-1-4992-0873-3

First edition

The author and publisher suggest consulting a health care professional should the reader have any questions regarding the information and material in this book. The author and publisher cannot be held responsible for any loss or claim arising out of the use, or misuse, of the preparations, materials or suggestions made, or the failure to take advice from a health care professional.

.

You were born with potential.
You were born with goodness and trust.
You were born with ideals and dreams.
You were born with greatness.
You were born with wings.
You are not meant for crawling,
You have wings...
Learn to use them and fly.

Jalal Uddin Rumi

CONTENTS

INTRODUCTION

The words here recount a time of two lives closely intertwined, living together in the moment and travelling afar in our learning.

As I entered motherhood with a tiny newborn in my arms, I knew that our first year would be momentous and extraordinarily special. I began with recounting my birth tale. Later, I found myself scribing each month, charting our story.

Our story attracted a following. People were drawn to my words, touched by the honest beauty of a new baby and curious about my natural food weaning approach.

With baby, the world revealed itself afresh. I noticed birds and flowers, rain and sun again, as if for the first time. With baby, I watched in wonder at the essence of our people; of happiness and laughter, of friendliness and energy, of suppleness and health.

I wrote whilst I was immersed in the novelty of each month. I was eager to depict the rapid growth of baby and recall the joys and lows of nurturing a natural child.

Pure Baby is a synthesis of monthly baby development and natural food and health insight. I infuse baby-led parenting and gentle sleep solutions with mind-body and Eastern medicine, the latest brain science and my personal experience.

1

PURE BABY

I conclude each chapter with a *Pure Baby Pearl* of guidance and wisdom, pertinent to the month. These pearls give you a collection of essential natural tools to strengthen the constitution of your baby.

A host of delicious recipes are located in the *Pure Baby Cookbook*, following the text. The repertoire of vital, nutritious dishes will nourish your health in pregnancy and as a new mother, and establish your baby's appetite for pure food.

The recipes and menu diaries from *First Food* onwards form a progressive programme to introduce solids to your little one, paced with the development of baby's digestive system.

I invite you to enter the lives of baby and I. Whether you are drawn to cooking, or delight in eating. Whether you are expecting a baby, or are already a parent. Whether you touch the lives of children, or of grown-ups. May you reap treasures from our story and may the *Pure Baby Pearls* shine to you.

PURE FOOD

Before becoming a mother, my dedication to good, honest food served me very well. I was fortunate to enter pregnancy in full health, and weave through the trimesters. I arrived at the final months feeling energised and supple, thanks to yoga, the power of the pregnancy hormone, *relaxin* and my whole foods eating.

My high regard for pure food first prepared my body for pregnancy, and then nourished the growing foetus in the womb. After the birthday, natural cuisine manifested as nutritious milk for baby, and later, accompanied us on a vibrant weaning journey.

My approach with food has a macrobiotic style. For me, this means high quality, organic food, plenty of plants and vegetables, whole ingredients and full, natural flavours. No sugar, processed components or artificial elements. I mark the seasons and enjoy the changing produce. I feel good eating this way, energised and clear, healthy and alive.

I apply macrobiotics in my kitchen by considering the energy of food and the creation of a balanced wholesome meal. I play with the two ancient forces of *yin* and *yang* in order to feed myself and nourish my new family.

I harmonise the open, light and fresh quality of yin with the concentrated, more compact energy of yang. This synchrony makes for a yummy, satisfying meal, nourishing all organs of the body and supporting their functioning.

I pay attention to the energy of foods I offer my baby. Her food welcomes new taste buds and motor skills, or induces calm pre-bed. Her meals uphold rapid growth and fuel her daily mastery of life.

This year, abundant cooking was overtaken by attending to baby, and relaxed conscious dining replaced by grabbing leftovers. The selfless nurturing of new life filled my days and nights.

Now it was about food fit for survival as a healthy mother, in between being grounded by nursing, summoned by baby's calls and playful games of peek-a-boo. Later in the year, food gained a new edge, as I nourished the constitution of the next generation, and weaning took flight with magic and delight.

PURE BABY PEARL
MACROBIOTICS IN A NUTSHELL

Macrobiotic eating sounds mysterious. Allow me to remove the mystery.

Macrobiotics brings honest ingredients and delicious foods together with Eastern medical wisdom to expand health.

Macrobiotic eating embraces the following three facets:

PURE FOOD

1. Flavour Full

Macrobiotics uses a host of delicious, pure and unrefined foods bursting with natural flavours and seasonings. The flavours in the food foster a feeling of perfect fullness, and this mitigates against grazing and post meal cravings. I will demonstrate how playing with the five key flavours of salty, sour, sweet, bitter and pungent is one trick to facilitate yummy nourishment.

2. Healthy Balance

Macrobiotic food is super healthy. Processed food, high salt and sugar contents and artificial components are replaced by fresh, whole foods and nutrient rich ingredients. Macrobiotic eating promotes a balanced diet, with plenty of plant based foods across an array of whole grains, beans, seasonal vegetables and even vegetables from the sea. If you wish, fish and quality animal produce can also be enjoyed.

3. Energetic Impact

Macrobiotics considers the qualities of ingredients and the effect food has on the body. Have you noticed that some foods make you feel energised and others make you more lethargic?

In oriental practices two energetic forces are present in every living thing. *Yin* is the feminine, upwards and opening energy, and *yang* is the male, downwards and contracting energy. The energetic properties of food can drive health and change mood, and also impact the vitality of body cells and organs.

Modern Macrobiotics

I regard macrobiotics as a powerful and integrated approach to life, which facilitates health, nourishment and vitality. Macrobiotics recognises each person's individuality and offers a bespoke and flexible eating style to anchor and expand health.

In *Pure Baby*, I distil my macrobiotic and natural food experience, and present vital information and guidance to give your baby a beautiful beginning.

PREGNANCY
THE FIRST
TRIMESTER

Tired Lethargy

New life has been building within me since the start of the year. I have watched the weeks wave and fall and a fresh sense of time has enveloped me. Time belongs to the innate natural cycles and beautiful timing carries life.

My approach has already changed. I relax, let go of anxieties, grow a mindfulness of my body and the tiny foetus I am carrying. I rest and lose my conscientious drive, overcome with this low, lethargic tiredness in months three and four.

Midnight Nibbles

My sense of smell heightens and nausea lodges in my throat. I no longer feel like nourishing myself and often refrain from cooking. Meals out, chips and sandwiches become necessary on several occasions. Mid night nibbles curb hunger in the quiet times.

7

Counting Weeks

Meanwhile, I count the weeks up until the public twelve week stage, only to be plunged into a very dark, private numbness.

My tiny baby receives tremendous risks for two life threatening conditions. I oscillate between undergoing the intrusive diagnostic tests of *chorionic villus sampling* and *amniocentesis*, and leaving nature to prevail. I write a poem entitled *Unconditional Love* and reflect on our life decisions.

UNCONDITIONAL LOVE: POETRY FROM THE WOMB

Do I really know of my baby's health for sure?
Am I facing this or striving past the seriousness?
Can I distinguish between my denial and my confidence?

I don't believe these numbers belong to us.
They are an anomaly.
Created by a computer, conjured to confuse and test our limits.
The risks remain in black and white, they will never fade.
I see them, I know them, yet I know not their mystery.

The pain and the fear and the turmoil and the talk and the tragedy.
But none of this is set in stone.
Please bring love to our baby.
Bring back the joy, the happiness and the celebration of this pregnancy.

PREGNANCY: THE FIRST TRIMESTER

Life is expanding millimetre by millimetre each day.
Our baby is dancing, playing and sleeping.
Our baby's genetics are set, DNA determining it's form over the coming
weeks and months.
Please bring love to our baby.

Unconditional love.
We love this baby yet we want it to be of perfect health.
Can we love unconditionally yet have such a preference?
Love means free from suffering according to the Buddhists.
So we love this baby and want us all to be free from suffering.

How will nature's generations treat us?
Do we wait and see, or do we find out now and multiply the risks?

Fear is finding out now.
Making choices from love not fear paves the doorways.
Love is finding out now.
Love to each other, confirmed love to the healthy baby.
Love to early knowing.

Fear pervades us if we don't find out now.
Love is respecting a healthy baby.
Love is respecting nature.
Love is respecting our partnership.

I ask for guidance, for help in making the best choice right now.
I ask for love for our baby and for nature to unfold kindness upon us.
Please give us the strength, the love and the perfect decision making.

9

I summon the strength to continue without gross intervention to my pregnancy and concrete knowledge of my baby's health. I submit to successive ultrasound scans instead.

PURE BABY PEARL
EATING FOR TWO

Slow & Small

Allow yourself to slow down, be lazy and have breakfast in bed. Give yourself rests and plenty of sleep opportunities. Eat small portions, regularly. Overeating diverts energy from the growing foetus to the digestive system instead.

Go Healthy

Stop sugar, alcohol and coffee. Go easy on tropical fruits and strong spices. Enjoy an array of different healthy food and reap the nutritious treasures from such a spectrum.

Morning Sickness

Rise slowly and have rice cakes handy. If you feel nauseous and can no longer enter the kitchen, perhaps someone can make you my delicious *Miso Minestrone* soup or a lovely pasta dish. Morning sickness and nausea generally subside post week thirteen.

PREGNANCY
THE SECOND
TRIMESTER

Preparing For Parenthood

Now at sixteen weeks, I allow myself to celebrate the pregnancy and begin to embrace all manner of classes to build my strength, flexibility, joy and insight into this incredible period. *Fit Bumps*, *Pregnancy Iyengar Yoga* and later *Active Birth* classes fill the agenda.

I delight in amassing wisdom that appeals to me in preparation for pregnancy, birth and parenthood. The *Birthlight Conference* I join, and with my husband make friends and form foundations together at the valuable *BabiesKnow* course.

Pure Portions

Suddenly I am getting used to eating smaller portions and dining more regularly. My morning appetite is much heartier, and by the evening my bump has swelled to a bloated pretence of a pregnant tummy.

11

PURE BABY

I make a concerted effort to digest a good diversity across my
pure food repertoire. I am keen on plant proteins, stocking up
on the protein and nutrient rich tempeh, alongside a variety of
lentils, adzukis, butterbeans and other pulses.

Grain Fuel

Whole grains I also give priority, and find some which please me
greatly. The high protein Aztec grains of quinoa and amaranth I
prefer. Also the sweet rice variety known as mochi, which is the
macrobiotic favourite grain in pregnancy and motherhood.
Mochi keeps the muscles elastic in preparation for birth, and
while breast feeding mochi, creates a sweet, nourishing milk.

Amidst the eastern energy dance of yin and yang, grains are the
most yang plant form. Grains carry more concentrated energy
than beans and pulses. Since pregnancy is a very yang
development of building new life, eating some yin foods fuel
harmony. With this understanding and following my natural
desires for certain foods, I became more and more aware of
eating in balance and my responsibility here to the growing baby
within.

Iron Veg

I go for generous servings of iron rich leafy greens fresh from
my organic delivery and often supplement dishes with
vegetables from the sea from local Irish waters. I widen my diet

to embrace the fish oils and protein from plenty of fish and also take on eggs for their complete amino acid complement.

Wheat & Fruit

I try to alleviate any sweet cravings with the introduction of baked butternut squash and longer cooked root vegetable dishes in my main meals. Fruit I do my best to have away from meals and I pass on wheat products as much as possible. Both foods create an uncomfortable bloated feeling for me.

PURE BABY PEARL
PREGNANCY NUTRITION

Iron Strong

Dose up on iron rich foods. Go for at least one serving of fresh, green vegetables daily. Their nutrient rich content will drive the quality of your blood and support your baby's development. Get friendly with kale, watercress and any other leafy greens. Sample my recipe for *Speedy Salt & Vinegar Greens*.

Iron strong foods also include pumpkin seeds and miso, tofu and tempeh, fish too. Vegetables from the sea such as nori and dulse. Whole grains and pulses, especially brown rice, barley and lentils. The *Gentle Lentil Dahl* is just divine and laden with iron.

Calcium High

You can generate your calcium intake from sources aside from dairy. Sesame seeds and tahini are rich in calcium. As are broccoli and leafy greens, vegetables from the sea, chickpeas and white beans, brown rice and quinoa. Try the *Quick Lemon Scented Quinoa Salad* for a nutritious lunch.

Nurture Yourself

Go outside, in nature. Surround yourself in beauty. After the first trimester has passed, begin preparing your body for birth. Partake in gentle exercise suitable for pregnancy. Send love and light to your growing baby every day.

PREGNANCY
THE FINAL
TRIMESTER

Pregnant Waves

I continue running cooking classes way into the depths of the third trimester. I feel good and normal, free from pain, and even free from any bloating which shadowed me over earlier weeks and months.

Now with only weeks to go I have a lovely pregnant tummy, shaping into mountains, which then become waves of movement. The delicate nudges make me giggle and fill with adoration.

Life In Limbo

I realise that this first pregnancy has been wonderful, special and healthy for me and I am very happy to have enjoyed such a positive experience. I become sad that this bump I have carried and which belongs to me will be no more in a few weeks time. I continue in a limbo between two lives and changing roles, and struggle to imagine how life will be beyond this summer.

15

Preparing For Birth

I am tending towards the light yin sweet foods. Perhaps this is a response to the great summer heat or a preparation for birth whereby such foods bestow relaxing and softening qualities on the uterus and birth canal. Women's legends also correlate sweet cravings in late pregnancy with the rich nectar of mother's milk.

I replenish my supplies of grains and seeds, tempeh and smoked tofu, sourdough breads and natural humous, beans and canned pulses too. Stocking up on handy nourishment for the weeks beyond birth when my impact in the kitchen will be far reduced.

I investigate receiving amasake, the fermented sweet rice delicacy that facilitates a beautiful quality of milk. I must also fill the freezer with homemade soups and stews.

The nursery is coming together. Fresh paint and borrowed furniture.

We await perfect timing for the arrival of our little one.

PURE BABY PEARL
HEARTY FLAVOURS

Heartburn

Eat small quantities and resist oily, greasy food. Absorb the stomach acid by chewing uncooked oat flakes thoroughly, before swallowing them. Enjoy pickles and pressed salads.

Rainbow Of Flavours

Using a variety of flavours in food is a powerful tool to keep you feeling nourished and satisfied. Try this method and see how it leaves you feeling perfectly full and mitigates against any cravings.

Do you remember the five key flavours? *Sweet, sour, salty, bitter* and *pungent*. Perhaps the last few flavours are lesser known. The trick is to combine two or more different flavours into your snack or meal. Visit the marinade in the *Secret Tempeh Stir Fry* to see how a host of different flavours are assembled.

Eating a rainbow of flavours will also prevent you from over-indulging on one food type. For example, if you like snacking on nuts, guard against over-eating this salty delicacy by enjoying fruit in combination. Dried fruit with seeds and nuts make a great balance of sweet and salty, or yin and yang.

PURE BABY

BIRTHDAY

The First Stage: Latent Phase

Labour began slowly for me. On Friday evening and the following day I felt like a teenager again skiving school for uncomfortable period pains. On Saturday, the long awaited *show* finally appeared whilst visiting one of Hampstead's sixteenth century stately homes! I was delighted and celebrated with a yummy South Indian meal at the magnificent *Neasden Temple* that evening. I was one week overdue already, with unwanted induction booked for the next Thursday.

By Sunday evening my tummy was tightening every seven minutes. Still I remained at the dinner table and jokingly monitored the intervals for each surge. Was this *Braxton Hicks*, *false labour* or the real thing? The contractions continued throughout Monday and I carried on as normal; doing the washing, shopping and cooking.

We made an epic journey to my acupuncturist in south London that afternoon in an attempt to speed up the labour and avoid medical induction. On arrival contractions were totally tolerable, yet every five minutes. Rush hour and the tube voyage home resulted in enormous relief to return safely.

The First Stage: Active Phase

We rushed through a meal, frantically finished packing the labour bags and although I was still in no pain, the contractions did interrupt my dinner this time. I felt ready to make another journey, to the hospital now.

One in the morning. As soon as I made the decision to leave, we quietly stole into a taxi amassed with luggage, minus the birthing ball however. Another momentous decision was to be made in the hospital lift. To opt for the natural and drug free birthing centre which I had been holding out for over the last nine months, or fall back to the labour ward.

I strolled into the birthing centre, with rucksack on my back. Greeted with the possibility I would be sent home. Yet, I was six centimetres dilated already and I wept in huge relief.

Aside from the quarter hourly monitoring of baby's heart beat and my pulse, we were left alone. The bean bag and later toilet seat quickly became my allies through the contractions. My husband too, massaging my back and navigating the music, was a secure support.

The First Stage: Transition

First, I longed to get into that birthing pool next door, the wails from the previous occupant I had already heard on arrival.

BIRTHDAY

Then, I cried to go home. Crazy pleas from a labouring woman mark the transition phase. This is the phase heralding full dilation and entry to the pushing part.

It must have been after four in the morning by the time I entered the birthing pool. The hot water was a wonderful pain relief, so much so that I laid my head back and actually slept in between the intense contractions. My husband too was sleeping and reawakening in tune with me.

The Second Stage: Birth

The surges swept me to my knees. Now, I abandoned the beautiful breathing techniques I had long practiced. The sensation to push remained and by half past six another examination finally found me fully ten centimetres dilated.

Staff shift change and two angels beckoned me out of the pool, relieved me since I hadn't passed water for the entire labour, and positioned me on the bed. With the slowest patience they allowed the baby's head to crown, and most happily avoided any great tearing or need for stitches.

At nine thirty-three that morning our baby was born.

The baby was clean, no vernix mucus overcoat. She was slight with long limbs and overgrown finger nails. Her left ear was folded from her passage to the world. Her eyes were open and she let out a quick healthy cry. Immediately she came to my chest. The umbilical cord had already stopped pulsing and this connection with me was clamped and severed.

The Third Stage

I felt sheer relief that the mammoth marathon to motherhood was over. Only delivery of the placenta was left. An hour is allocated for this vital organ to be naturally expelled. Fifty five minutes later, the placenta plopped out fully intact, thankfully.

Now the midwives tenderly cleaned up and weighed our precious new being. Six pounds and twelve ounces, certainly a healthy weight.

PURE BABY PEARL
INGREDIENTS FOR BIRTH

Pre-Birth

I prepared for the birth by listening to the beautiful *Jeyarani Way's Birth Rehearsal Visualisation.*

Labour

Background music from *Comfort Zone* created a gentle atmosphere. The essential oil of Clary Sage carries a very potent aroma which brought me enormous sensory relief amidst contractions.

Two large cartons of vitalising coconut water were a welcome hydrating fluid throughout the labour. The presence and support of my husband was invaluable and his back massages were most welcome during the contractions.

Post-Birth

My mother's home made brown rice sushi following the delivery was perfect. In the days after the birth, baths with sea salts were brief moments of bliss!

PURE BABY

WELCOME BABY

I am in love again. I look at her and my heart melts. I just want to view her all the time. I keep discovering her features. Yesterday I noticed her perfect little ankle. Today I delight in stroking her hair soft as silk, and skin which carries the gentle texture of water.

I smile and delight in all her appearances. Her gaze beckons beyond me. Her arms make sudden jerky movements or tuneful waves as if conducting an orchestra. Frequent sneezes and hiccups resonate through her entire body.

As she feeds I watch each angle of her peaceful, elegant face. When the feed comes to a close, her eyelids shut and head turns from side to side with her nose pointed high. This is her beautiful face high on the nectar of my hind milk; the latter milk rich in calories.

In her deep angelic sleep, she murmurs and often places her head towards the right, her arms up high with fingers pointing in an array of directions.

Welcome Jemima Ella.

PURE BABY

MONTH 1
NEWBORN
NOVELTY

Fuelling New Skills

We return from the secure stay in hospital. Jemima sleeps and eats and we marvel at how contented she is over that first week. We dine amidst a growing mass of pink cards and regular visitors in our living room.

With each day I notice new features, more beauty and the world afresh as if I have been reborn myself. For the first ten days I am delicate and sore and hardly venture outside. Suddenly on the eleventh day I feel significantly better. Yet for the newborn, now the cries are louder, suck stronger and contented blissful state no longer a fixture.

I delight in nappy changes and cuddles, yet I dread feeding times. Her feeding causes me pain, and by weeks two and three, early evening feeding stretches late into the night. This tiresome new skill creates many questions. Breast feeding specialists and health visitors pacify me that frequent, even continual, feeding is normal. Yet, speaking to a new mum grants me the greatest comfort at this challenging stage, a phase I am promised shall pass.

PURE BABY

I am hugely fortunate to be very well looked after. I simply show up for meals or I am served great spreads whilst I feed the little princess. In a strange sense, it feels like being on holiday. I enjoy all the meals and snacks and many drinks, since breast feeding is a hungry, thirsty business.

Now the feeding is established. Little Jemima knows her mother. My scent and safety are familiar to her. Feeding times easily take an hour, and I am hesitant to de-latch baby before she is satisfied. For several days we have intervals of four hours between feeds, other days feeds are far more frequent. Most evenings I am glued to the feeding chair and on the rare occasion I make it downstairs, I feel a huge freedom.

Sometimes she feeds and squirms like a little animal, agitated wind interrupting her flow. Other times peaceful drinking fuels her adorable milk drunk routine. Suddenly milk spots interrupt her smooth skin, move elsewhere across her cheeks and then disappear.

It's just over three weeks in and I make the mammoth journey to my local baby weigh in. Hours are consumed in preparation for any excursion. Infact, even without excursions the days with baby travel too quickly.

The scales leave me feeling fully contented with our feeding habits. I am in awe at her rapid expansion and in nostalgic disbelief that the precious newborn days are already over. Now I see the eight pounds, five ounces in her rounded cheeks and tummy, her filled out and oversized fingers and feet.

MONTH 1: NEWBORN NOVELTY

Windy Nights

Countless times, I realise that there are no short cuts with
newborns. A nappy change now does not negate the need for a
nappy change later. Similarly, a speedy feed now will not bypass
another feed shortly. Plus, a quick feed results in a vast quantity
of air ingested and an unhappy, windy baby.

Many a night I struggle helplessly with the symptoms of horrible
colic. The rigid legs and sheer discomfort. The relentless
feeding and reluctant sleep. My memory fades and only the
previous night impresses upon my joy of motherhood.

Another mighty trip takes us to the *Craniosacral* therapist at
Violet Hill Studios. Jemima's first treatment to dispel any trauma
from the birth. She lies over two pillows and remains in the
most beautiful sleep over the course of her session. The
practitioner moves from baby's feet to crown and realigns the
inner fluids and membranes. Jemima has very little tension it
turns out. She stays sleeping long afterwards, and the scars of
colicky nights certainly dwindle in the days to follow.

First Contact

Jemima begins to look at me and connect her eyes to mine.
Then she is looking at a soft toy and reaching out in touch.
From the blank gaze beyond me to such focused attention fills
me with delight. She is concentrating on the black and white
images, how wonderful! And in the next second her mouth

widens, her head reddens and her eyes scrunch up. Louder cries project from her little body.

Baby's nature alters in an instant. Baby knows no separation from me. My mood is her being, and my love and fatigue shape her spirit.

PURE BABY PEARL
INGREDIENTS FOR NEW MUMS

New Mum's Meals

Baby is all consuming. My nourishment feels vital to restore strength following the birth and in order to generate good milk for the little one. I am so lucky to be served home cooked, abundant, wholesome meals this month. I enjoy plenty of soups and sweet rice, rich fish and gentle fried dishes, cooked and baked vegetables. Oh and the weekly takeaway!

Two tips for nourishment in the early days:

1. **Forego Bubbly**

    For the first ten days particularly, forego celebratory champagne and simple sugars. Sugar can exaggerate deficiency after giving birth and deplete your energy. Seek good quality sweet flavours from ground and root vegetables and pure puddings sweetened with rice syrup or other alternatives to sugar. Satisfy your sweet tooth naturally with a delicious *Cosy Fruit Plate*.

2. **Go Mineral Rich**

   Go for mineral rich foods and miso to aid the contraction of your uterus back to a normal size. Enjoy strengthening dishes such as thick soups and include fish and hearty stews. Encourage someone to prepare you a rich *Surprise in a Soup* or *Miso Minestrone*, *Secret Tempeh Stir Fry* or *Wholesome Millet Menu*.

Nursing Know How

There are several options for feeding your baby. Be at peace with the style you select, as this serves you right now.

If you go with breast feeding, know that it is a new skill for you and baby. Perhaps you are automatically adept or you try hard in vein. Seek local breast feeding support or *lactation consultants* for encouragement and guidance. Consider what you are eating and give yourself enough rest.

Four essential ingredients for nursing:

1. Milk Flow

Milk normally begins flowing on the second or third day after the birth. Nourishment and rest are the forerunners to milk manufacture, and stress and activity are the barriers. Feeding baby is critical to stimulate milk production. Light dishes, steamed cooking styles and fennel tea can help support the generation of milk, if it is not yet flowing.

2. Your Baby Is What You Eat

Breast fed babies reflect what you are eating. Clean eating and drinking upholds a pure baby. Enjoy well cooked whole grains, particularly oat groats and mochi rice. Have nourishing porridges such as my *New Mums Congee Deluxe* to support the production of your milk.

Sugar and fruit juices, baked flour and cheese consumed by mum can contribute to excess mucus production in the little one. Beware of certain foods too which can aggravate the delicate digestive systems of newborns and result in colic and other symptoms in your baby. Read more on *Calming Colic & Wind* in *Month 2*.

3. Perseverance and Surrender

I found it hard to comprehend that baby was still hungry when one feed merged with the next. However, as the cries and routing persisted, I let baby lead the feeding routine in these early weeks. By month end, feeds without gaps were gone, and sustainable feeds appear to be mastered.

4. Cabbage

Not for eating, since vegetable members of the cruciferous family are no allies of colic and wind in babies. However, the application of cabbage leaves are the age old remedy to soothe sore nipples and it works!

Pace and Rest

I take my time to venture outside and stay at home for more than ten days. Resting helps my milk production. In the east, new mothers remain indoors for several weeks after childbirth during their *golden month*. I like my slow return to vague normality. To honour the new being and these special, precious early days. It is widely acknowledged that post natal depressions are rife when life is resumed too quickly.

PURE BABY

MONTH 2
SOUNDS & SMILES

Morning has broken and we are a few days into the second month. I receive an unmistaken, beautiful smile from Jemima as she awakens. I ooze with pride. The smile has been brewing over the last week or so. Now I can knowingly broadcast Jemima's beam, without a worry for that windy grin whose facade she wore in former weeks.

Week Five

Halfway through week five and suddenly some feeds have hastened to ten minutes in duration. Wind becomes more of a nuisance now. Intervals between night feeds are ranging from two to five hours. She begins forcing her right fist into her mouth and sucking on the fingers of this hand.

I re-enter the kitchen and make my first soup since baby arrived, a quick thick parsnip number. This week we also enjoy an evening out at my favourite cosy Thai place. Jemima hurls a wail as the hat overthrows her eyes on the journey there. I learn that her cries really do communicate necessities. And I figure that patience is Jemima's first quality to surface, since she gently awaits our attempts to understand and satisfy her needs.

Once the hat resumes its position, she is back sleeping. She remains sleeping though the cold and all the transfers, but does not permit me to relax entirely on our first evening's excursion. A feed mid way through our meal is on the menu of course.

Week Six

The six week doctors' visit heralds Jemima as ten pounds in weight. A movement on the growth charts from the twenty fifth to the fiftieth percentile. Now we switch from the occasional *swaddle* blanket to the daily *Gro sleeping bag*. The sleeves of her first baby grow, which once totally submerged her arms, now no longer fit. I wash this early outfit to save for a brother or sister, and I feel sad that my baby is tiny no more. I struggle to even visualise her newborn features and remember her early self.

I sign up for several mum and baby classes. It feels good to be resuming some normality, targeting the day with making the session's start, and filling the day with returning home again.

The baby massage class Jemima and I love. Her head sits cradled between my feet and she gazes at me maintaining eye contact and pursing her lips in connection throughout. Post natal Pilates and fitness we also join to restore my pelvic tone.

I am delighted with my new *Maclaren* pushchair of the *Quest Sport* style. I spend my walking hours lost in thought over its nimble agility and light mastery. Such are the sentiments of a new mum. Gone are my clumsy, heated attempts to construct and deconstruct the weighty *iCandy*.

My head aches of exhaustion from feeding every two hours over the last few evenings. I feel helplessly frustrated at having no time off over the last seven weeks, spare my husband's trip to the local shops with baby in *Bjorn*. I can't complete a thing, a laundry load takes all day. I feel incompetent at being able to do any domestic chores.

Frustration too seeps within me over my birth experience. More and more I am dismayed by the prolonged and painful affair. Surely, if I had been permitted to push when I had longed to, my birth account would have been half as long and far less agonising.

Week Seven

Now Jemima is seven weeks old and we explore tummy time. On her front, her legs rhythmically make crawling movements, yet she stays in the same spot. Her head lifts and the effort brings sounds and a directed gaze. That tummy time aids the head and brain development, must be true.

Another new position Jemima and I relish is the bouncer chair. Here, she reclines above ground level now, and can view the room and its activities. She kicks and thrusts her arms about in a wonderful state of quiet alertness. And I may commence some of the things I was feeling so inadequate about last week.

Preparing dinner is one of those activities. Last night I cooked a meal while daddy bathed and then coaxed the little one to sleep. I rush through eating and any other non baby thing in anticipation of being needed, summoned to provide care.

Twice this week, explosions fill baby's nappy and spread up to her shoulders, without a warning. Jemima appears non fussed about a nappy change, and less so about these delayed motions. I understand her digestion and assimilation of my milk is improving, and irregular poos are the prize.

Week Eight

The cluster feeds encompassing late afternoon and evening, which were a fixture earlier this month, have dissolved. Now paced gaps filter through into the remains of the day. Overnight, I celebrate the rare six hour intervals and berate the two hourly gaps between feeds.

We begin *Baby Sensory* sessions. Wide eyes and curiously alert, Jemima is keen on the songs and matching signs. She seems to notice the other children too. Back at home, her whole face smiles at repetitions of the rhymes.

Express Train

I try my hand at expressing, with an electric kit however. I am horrified at how my loving feeding ritual is replaced by such a mechanical sterile business. This could be training for an undisturbed night, yet the intention backfires and we are all up for hours that evening. Jemima takes the bottle but cries for more than the extracted two ounces of my precious milk.

Mastitis Misery

I realise I am enjoying the breast feeding. Holding my baby close, the precious moments are smitten with tenderness and love. These times have fuelled our symmetry. I am attuned to Jemima and I strive to attend to her hunger before she utters a howl.

However, today I awake cold, my whole body aches and weeps with lack of heat and energy. Feeding Jemima is painful, I feel sore and bruised. Every movement hurts. A fever erupts and *mastitis* takes its residence. I remain in bed, my first good rest since pre birth. Jemima in empathy, stays contented throughout the day.

Tomorrow my temperature is back to normal and *blocked milk ducts* assert their presence. I listen to my body and continue to rest, cancelling clients' cooking and classes.

Macrobiotics deems mastitis as a reflection of over activity. Indeed, since week six I had been rushing to postnatal classes, pram pushing for miles and adding to my pressure with responding to prospective emails. I stop all this exertion and silently stay at home.

Fingers And Hums

Jemima's boxer's fist is loosening now. The fingers are unfurling and then grabbing on my hair and relaxing again by her side. She supports her head so much better now. Her honest eyes attend to mine like an adhesive, glued to my every move. Legs splash out in excitement and arms continue to conduct the orchestra.

Beautiful noises and fresh tones sparkle from her voice every day. The music of my baby is beginning with all the vowel sounds. Later the consonants will gather pace. Her inflections speak to me, telling me of her pure delight and drawing me near. When the pitch lowers to a frustrated moan, I hear her signals for a change in scenery.

PURE BABY PEARL
NATURAL MEDICINE

Calming Colic & Wind

The mother's consumption of wheat, dairy and beans are common causes of colic and wind. Garlic, onions and cabbage are further contributors. I also found raw foods were not friendly for baby.

For us, in the early days, evenings following eating adzuki beans were riddled with colicky distress. Welcome, even invite anyone to prepare food for you! Be sure to suggest they use a small strip of kombu sea vegetable when cooking beans, as this seaweed offsets effects of gas.

Give yourself time to burp baby well after each feed. Baby massage is a beautiful aid to relax baby and there are certain routines which help alleviate colic and gas. Hot towels on baby's tummy also provide comfort.

Reflux

Here baby's stomach is tight and this prevents milk from descending down the gut. Vomiting, coughing and distress result. For the breastfeeding mum, address what you are eating and be careful about heavy baked goods, excess meat and dairy.

Mastitis Recovery

Rest in bed was a huge remedy for me. The *rugby ball hold* feeding position allowed baby to continue feeding from the affected side and receive milk from clear ducts. Hot towels, massage and plenty of nursing helped the blocked ducts soften. I eat steamed daikon, a macrobiotic wonder vegetable from the radish family, and dose up on homeopathic *Phytolacca*.

PURE BABY

MONTH 3
BABY KNOWS

The week is ten, the eye contact is strong, legs and arms spray and the two way raspberries crescendo. In slow motion a smile appears and baby's mouth broadens. Behold, the first chuckle gathers pace.

Head And Shoulders

For a few weeks since my mastitis, Jemima has lost interest in tummy time. We persevere and by week twelve, she is more content on her front. On the last day of this week, she unexpectedly begins holding her head up while lying in this pre crawling position. Her legs move excitedly but she travels nowhere.

Neck strength and head control are much more impressive now. Jemima revolves her head to survey the room, smiles and converses with herself about the surroundings.

She regards her hands with great attention and is fascinated by outstretching her arms to hail and greet me. She resumes this position purposefully; the direction of her arms is no longer accidental. The swipes of her hands at items are being replaced by targeted tugs of my hair and the turning of toys.

Sleeping Like A Baby

Now that the feeding is fine, I try to understand sleep. At first I feel that Jemima is resisting sleep, preferring to stay awake and play. Here, she would enter another two hour cycle before she may be tired again.

Perhaps she isn't fighting sleep, but it is me who is out of tune with her ideal moment for bed. I learn over many days and nights to spot her signs of fatigue. I attempt to heed the prophesy of the early yawns and rubbing of eyes. The tired wail is a later signal, and I recognise that her brief outburst on the brink of sleep dictates a slumber.

The morning nap is established. Two hours after rising, Jemima is tired again. She sleeps for one baby sleep cycle of thirty five minutes and no longer! A pattern is emerging for the rest of the day. Two hour wakeful cycles can sandwich a lunchtime nap and afternoon siesta. Each day is wildly variable however, and my excursions and activities impact Jemima's rhythm.

I do notice the nights when bedtime is perfectly timed to Jemima's behaviour and a relaxed affair. Then, Jemima's first stretch of sleep is so much longer than on those evenings when bed is battled and surpassed by overtiredness. I generally make preparations for bed in anticipation of Jemima's sudden tiredness by half past six. Bath, massage, baby grow, feed. I am connecting these activities with bedtime in the hope that baby is too!

Baby Knows

For several days in week thirteen, Jemima sleeps for hours at a time and feeds more regularly at night. Post this growth spurt I view my daughter afresh. Her fleshy thighs and silky skin, her charming laughter and eyes deeply alive. Her honest interest and disposition of purity. My once delicate, unknowing baby is becoming robust and aware. Her conscious actions, smiles and sounds are building her being. My manner, approach and style are shaping her spirit.

PURE BABY PEARL
BABY YIN YANG

I look at Jemima and I try to determine the quality of her constitution and her energy. How can I apply my work with yin and yang to my little daughter? Her body feels strong and present, bold and alive. A yang attribute here. Yet her nature is gentle and accepting, a softer yin within. Later she will assert her strong will, her yang desire to remain on the swings or eat more food.

I observe her physical traits. She sleeps tenderly on her back with arms sprayed out. Her body is open now, unlike inside the womb, the tight, folded, yang foetus of a few weeks ago. Her cries feel harmless and without tears.

PURE BABY

She is dainty and patient, safe and peaceful, tolerant and trusting. She is content and happy being here and I am overjoyed by her presence.

I feel blessed with a balanced and happy baby; all the energies of heaven and earth appear in harmony.

MONTH 4
LITTLE PERSON

Feeding Woes

The three to four month *sleep regression* is causing longer and more frequent feeds at night than during daytime. Jemima is too busy being curious in her awake periods to take any interest in feeding in the day. She will begin feeds and quickly disembark, distracted by light or clothing or anything which her eyes attend to. Her previous long night stretches of sleep are replaced by periods of two hours. Again, I acknowledge that with baby, nothing is a permanent, everything changes.

For several days, she moans and as with the newborn haze, the hours pass with many changes in position and effortful attention. Bubbles and dribble ooze from her mouth, and her cheeks are flushed. All signs of the challenging times of teething.

Bath & Bed

Suddenly bath time is less bewildering. She seems to have discovered her legs and feet over the last few days. Now she begins to thrust her legs about in the bath. Her monkey toes cling to the sides and even hold onto duck between her two feet. Her arms soften and hands open and smiles emerge.

Bed time associations appear to be blooming. She rubs her eyes and lets out her sleepy wail post bath and massage. I start to introduce *Snuggle Bunny*, a bed time story. The front cover of which stimulates her very much for a few seconds, before tiredness overcomes her and feeding beckons instead.

First Sight

Her face is fresh with interest as her eyes behold things for the very first time. Her mouth concentrates and she makes sounds of delight and smiles of pleasure. Her sounds are a little lower now; the high pitched non human tone has been replaced by softer 'm' sounds of beautiful varieties.

Jemima does definitely see and even smile at other babies. Her legs move with excitement as she notices new environments. And when she feels relaxed, the most beautiful conversations vocalise.

Mum's Measures

My mind is deep with *baby brain*. My concern and attention is only for Jemima. I kick myself for lack of thought for others and moments of memory loss. My sharpness elapses and any broad thinking is banished.

MONTH 4: LITTLE PERSON

I manage ad hoc expressing with hunched shoulders, neck ache and utter dislike. Jemima drinks less than half the ounces while I teach full cooking classes.

Baby On Board

I am warned that travelling with baby will entail the same daily demands, yet in a differing location. Remove any expectation of a holiday. We board the plane amidst heavy snow. Jemima appears to thrive on this new journey experience. Air pressure and aircraft speed cause her no dissatisfaction.

We arrive to sun. How will baby adapt to this new climate and setting? Infact the new environment pleases her greatly. She rotates her head one hundred and eighty degrees and bobbles her chin to take in all the new surroundings. She smiles and chuckles with all the family members, and eats and sleeps at all good opportunities. She takes to the water too.

For me, the week is certainly a new experience as well. Gone is the freedom to explore and partake in any crazy excursion. Now, my chief priority is caring for Jemima, and a speedy swim or relaxing bath are the baby-free specials of my holiday.

Little Person

The day we return home Jemima turns four months.

PURE BABY

A week ago we took our little baby to a new country and climate. Now she comes home, a developing whole person, mastering many milestones. She has grown before my eyes. The wardrobe of gifts of three to six month old clothes will not see much more wearing.

She discovered her thighs, knees and feet. Jemima has been surveying her legs as she holds them upwards in the air, or stroking her limbs with now open palms. Her hands are hardly held in tight fists any longer. The dexterity of her fingers has flourished overnight. She is holding toys, gripping onto items and folding her ears. She is sucking her thumb and her mouth welcomes the world through taste.

She is smiling and sounding high pitched squeals of pleasure. When she meets others, especially children and babies, her eyes widen and she happily converses using adorable expressions and tones. She is looking at everything now and learning so much about our sociable species, about how we live and how we interact.

I watch as suddenly this complete little person becomes aware of herself and her limbs, and of the people and places around her. I respect her and recognise and respond to her wonderful inquisitiveness and beautiful bewilderment.

PURE BABY PEARL

KIND CONNECTIONS

I am fascinated that at birth, my baby's brain had shoals of neurons but they were without connections. Her capacity and potential was mammoth.

She could acquire any language or species sound. Infact, right now her tunes are that of birdsong. Her traits and qualities, skills and hobbies could be limitless. Her ways and values, with exposure, could be lifted from another culture or community. Equally, she will quickly lose these vast possibilities, since without use such brain cells will cease to exist.

The synapses are fusing and neural pathways are being determined. I see the motor connections firing with the progression of her coordination. I know that how I respond to her, sets up the pattern of her nervous system now and for the future.

If Jemima is dealt with kindness, interaction and response, will she see the world with warmth and allow those neurons facilitating friendship and love to flourish? Indeed, Jemima's brain will connect affection with movement of the arms, and manifest her trademark waves of greeting.

If anxiety and stress prevail, pathways may be stimulated, that dictate the flooding of cells by cortisol. This hormone of stress could become a fixture if such pathways are repetitively trodden.

51

PURE BABY

Stress tenses the body, tightens the organs, impacts on digestion and is the prelude to all manner of poor health.

MONTH 5
POWER OF NOW

Present Prevails

For baby, the present prevails. She exists right now, in her cheeky smile and lovely laugh, her curiosity and frustration, her hunger or her fatigue. For me with baby, nothing else matters and I cherish the moment alive with her.

I love seeing her wide eyes, beautifully alert. The whites are the clearest colour, unmarred and totally pure. Soft shades surround her knowing pupils. She does not avert her gaze and enjoys long eye contact.

Appetite Control

Jemima loses her appetite during the day, and is exercising choice over when she feeds. Unfortunately for me, she chooses night over day and therefore I continue to arise twice overnight. Her appetite control is very apparent now. Sometimes she indicates lack of hunger at a feeding time dictated by me. Nevertheless, a short while later, hunger can often return.

For a week or more, Jemima is off her food. Her motions turn green and runny, perhaps a result from my excess attempts at offering her breast milk. Her spirit remains strong and soon she is feeding better once more. Now I feed on her signal, her noisy cue which indicates hunger and is good guarantee of a full feed. At home, I return to the same spot for feeding which she recognises and serves as a ploy to reduce any distraction.

Monologue Of Nattering

She parades a new look. Here, her tongue is poised out of her mouth as she takes great interest in things for the first time. Now she is mimicking our kisses and blowing raspberries. She purses her lips together and sounds a kiss, and delights in these kissing conversations.

As she approaches five months of age, she is stringing sounds together. Her gentle talking greets other babies, often with a monologue of nattering.

Energy Exchange

Jemima spends many opportunities examining her hands and feet. She notices each finger then uses her hands to stroke, grab and scratch away. Her toes have similar dexterity to her fingers. She spreads each toe wide apart, and fashions her feet to pick up items.

Jemima has become much more mobile, but still travels nowhere. On her front, she is raising her head high with arms outstretched. She uses her legs to force her bottom up in the air and pushes backwards just a little. And on her back she wriggles, arching her middle and lifting her legs.

I marvel at her insatiable energy. The energy from my milk transformed into the rapid growth and development of a complete, conscious being within weeks. How the speed of nature, and the flawless beauty of babies work in harmony.

PURE BABY PEARL
TRUE HEALTH

I feel so blessed and grateful for Jemima's beautiful health. How fortunate she is to live without struggle, with all her needs met. She seems to simply love being here, she appears to love life.

I am reminded that true health is not the absence of dis-ease, but the capacity to embrace life. The word macrobiotics, indeed, means the *big life*, the living of a rich life.

I marvel at the innate health of a baby, the yearning for fun and spirit for life. The sheer wonder and effortless learning, the profound energy and affinity with nature. How can we carry these qualities of true health beyond childhood?

PURE BABY

MONTH 6
FIRST FOOD

Face Plants

For a few days Jemima perfects the sound *dada* by repeating it over and over, much to my husband's delight, but less so in the middle of the night! Then she proceeds onto new noises, practicing a range of sounds that resonate like sentences.

The suppleness of a baby is astonishing. Overnight she progresses from touching her feet to sucking her toes. Then she is waving her arms about in excitement and making accidental rolls of her body. Now she is making early attempts to crawl backwards. As month six approaches she begins sitting with an enviously perfect straight back and awkward balance. The first tears ensue as face plants and nose dives follow.

Suddenly daytime naps persist past the accustomed thirty five minute threshold. The variety of the nap period and occurrence still leaves me with minimal baby free opportunity. Besides, longer awake periods have also arisen.

Face Wide Smiles

Jemima's attention span is quite apparent now. She diligently attends to something, focusing all her concentration in that moment. I marvel at her lasting durations of absolute intent. However, upon interaction with people, often her whole face oozes with smiles and sheer joy. She thrives off the banter with others, the physical play and the rhythm of the nursery rhymes.

She captivates with her pure joy, charms with her face wide smiles and sense of fun. But her laughter is the most beautiful. She beckons us to share in this true happiness, and we play plenty of games to generate another fantastic giggle.

First Meal

Thus far Jemima has only consumed breast milk, her ideal fuel which matches it's nutritional make up to her growing demands. She has managed her consumption and filled out to become a fleshy baby.

Now I gear up for weaning, reflecting on the *puree* style and *baby led* approach. I read and speak to others, and opt for the two methods since the benefits of both appeal to me.

Baby's digestive system is young and only accustomed to milk which can be readily assimilated. Graduating to the gentle introduction of soft, tender soup-like foods makes sense as the next step.

MONTH 6: FIRST FOOD

At the same time, baby's dexterity, coordination and development is taking mammoth leaps. She is looking at me during meal times, mimicking chewing movements with her mouth, and yearning to be involved. She focuses on holding items and moving them between her fingers, and is progressing to using the *pincer grip*.

I begin to give her cooked florets of broccoli, carrot chunks and green beans to play with and become familiar with such food. The irony of this initial baby led play with vegetable pieces is that none enter the mouth. Of course all other items get saturated with saliva as the mouth tastes the world.

I hold off the first *Baby Rice Milk* until I can no longer bear dining in front of Jemima. At this point she is a week away from six months old and a mere day away from sitting. I prepare her momentous first meal with great care and attention, even though I have made my own grain milk countless times before. In true macrobiotic style, I pressure cook short grain brown rice and sweet rice with seven times as much water. Then using a sieve I separate the soft rice from the cream.

I serve her the rice cream in a cup and she beckons for more than a few sips. A result! I watch her digestive system that day and the next. My second attempt is less successful. Her excitement at breakfast quickly dissipates as she finds the food too hot, and she withdraws at lunchtime in memory of my hopeless earlier attempt.

Right now her digestive system and gut flora are perfect, untarnished by any foul food or toxicity. Can I preserve this perfection and uphold her healthy vigour through weaning and beyond?

BABY RICE MILK

The idea of preparing your own rice milk is most certainly a *Pure Baby Pearl*, glistening among your wholesome toolkit. Homemade rice milk confers all the nutrition of whole grains as an easily digestible drink. Rice milk is most nourishing for baby and can also be enjoyed by all the family. I often use this wonderful tonic to thicken soups and make creamy sauces. Here is baby's first recipe.

Ingredients:

1 cup whole grains (eg. half cup short grain brown rice and half cup sweet mochi rice)
7 cups water
Pressure cooker or heavy pan with a lid
Sieve or food mill

Preparation:

Rinse the grains and place in the pan. Add the water and leave the grains to soak for three hours or overnight. Then put the pan on a medium flame, cover with a lid and bring to the boil. If you are using a pressure cooker, bring this up to pressure. Reduce the heat and cook for one hour to one hour and a half.

Now transfer the contents of the pan to a sieve over a bowl and stir the mixture through the sieve. Alternatively use a food mill here. The resulting extracted liquid is grain milk. This can be stored in the fridge for 3 days.

Variations:

As baby grows, I play with the consistency of the milk in three ways. First, I gradually reduce the amount of water added to the pan with successive weeks. Secondly, I stir the grain through the sieve with some vigour in order to create a nourishing and thick rice cream. Finally, I achieve an array of nutrition and taste by cooking a variety of grains in combination. I use two or three different varieties from selections of brown rice, millet, oat groats, sweet rice, pot barley and more.

PURE BABY

MONTH 7
PURÉE V BABY LED

Sunrise

As day breaks, Jemima salutes the sun with her beautiful baby sounds. One morning as the sun meets our cutlery and makes a dance of light on the ceiling, she is following these rays above before we notice them at all. She is acutely aware of noises and attunes to the direction of birdsong, cars and aircraft overhead.

She sculpts my face with her fingers in a display of affection and gives others big, wet kisses as she tastes the world. She is nattering and smiling in groups now, particularly those with a relaxed setting and atmosphere. Laughter is guaranteed in games that copy her sounds and movements, or playoffs of peek-a-boo.

She is enjoying sitting up, playing and talking to herself and her toys. I am enjoying spectating. She summons great effort in picking up objects and moving them between her fingers, and then reaching out for toys afar and sitting back upright. She takes pleasure in sitting upright in her pram, supporting herself throughout rocky journeys, and engaging with the local streets and residents.

Baby Rice

I am using different grains to prepare *Baby Rice Milk* varieties around twice a week. Jemima is readily accepting these and is hovering the lot. She has progressed from dining on a mere teaspoon to a good few tablespoons over perhaps two weeks. We have certainly hit a new phase since her stools have thickened. Her digestion of the new food seems very good indeed.

Yesterday's cocktail of brown rice, sweet rice and pot barley she liked very much. I am adding five times as much water so the texture is thick and creamy now. The remaining soft grain is being transformed into a celebrated dish. My *Mummy Rice Pudding* recipe intended as a nourishing treat for mums engaged in weaning, is being enjoyed by family members and friends alike.

Veggies Two Ways

The vegetables Jemima is not as fond of as the rice milk. The first mouthful of anything always generates this monstrous look of disgust, and then her head reaches forward for more. Carrot, butternut squash and sweet potato she goes for a few spoonfuls, and courgette and parsnip purees she passes. For the next attempt, I mix the vegetable puree with the grain milk and craft a meal which is better received.

After a good few weeks of play with vegetables, Jemima is putting the carrot chunks in her mouth and extracting some goodness with her sucking. I quickly learn that a meal must follow the order of puree first, baby led second course. Beginning with the baby led technique creates too much distraction for the second style to be effective.

Purée v Baby Led

In the puree approach, she gets very excited and thrusts her head forward in anticipation of food. She can hold the spoon and is also using the cup to drink. With assistance, she can easily engulf a good few tablespoons of rice milk now.

With baby led, dining is a different story. Here, dining is about discovery, play with food, fascination with texture and movement. Jemima's first encounter with broccoli was a long marvel of picking up the florets, pushing them around her tray and raising a few to her mouth. Baby led weaning is not about filling the stomach at this stage.

The Greeting

Now Jemima is actively seeking me out and I am receiving heart melting, beaming smiles from her. In groups, she is noticing my presence and smiles as she turns around to see me. The separation anxiety may be setting in however, and she can get a little unsettled by my absence.

She lurches forward and cocks her head to see round corners. She sees me from afar in a room full of people. She is laughing to get my attention. Now she is breathing deeply in concentration, mouth gaping in wonder and head peering round to get a better view.

Then she is reaching out to stroke another baby or gently admire my fingers. Next she is waving her hands in excitement, perhaps in desire of a feed.

Today, upon leaving grandma, she turned her hand in a waving motion, mimicking our daily gesture for the very first time. Tomorrow and the days that follow she has great fun greeting others with her new wave. She reaches out one hand also, inviting people to meet her with touch.

She is understanding our days, comprehending our ways. She is fully engrossed in absorbing living.

PURE BABY PEARL
MUMMY LOVE

Indulge in this luxurious skin tonic and enjoy a yummy *Mummy Rice Pudding*. Savour a moment for yourself.

Skin Kind

My upper arms were marred with spots after child birth, and I found skin brushing provided a luxurious skin tonic. Skin brushing acts to exfoliate the skin and dramatically helps the circulation and movement of the lymph.

A moist skin brush is used over the skin, particularly on all four limbs, before showering. Your skin will become a little pink upon brushing, and after bathing will feel beautifully soft. Do be gentle if your skin is sensitive.

PURE BABY

MONTH 8
DOUBLE GREETING

Green Soups

I am making purees of mixed vegetables, searching for ingredients Jemima will like. The purees also serve as great salt free soups for us. I persevere with the traditional first foods of orange coloured vegetables, but then discover that Jemima is far fonder of greens than that of carrot and squash.

Her face turns green as she delights in a neat spinach puree. Then I prepare combinations of courgette, fennel, Chinese cabbage and dill which she appears to enjoy. My *Green Baby Soup* and another soup of cauliflower, watercress, and onion are readily received.

Mean Sleeps

Soon butternut squash and carrot become palatable. Then a night of teething takes hold and some days later Jemima's whole mouth and chin area are scorched in an unsightly red.

Sleep patterns are changing. When she hit seven months old, she fell asleep with ease in her cot and then awoke twice during the night. Now she is remaining very awake in her cot as the day closes and night time awakenings are persisting.

Hidden Learning

Jemima has taken to sliding on wooden floors. One arm now extends and discovers all manner of table legs, cupboards, feet and shoes at this ground level.

She is amassing much pleasure in play, like a little girl already. Taking her hat off, pulling at leaves, poking buttons, and hiding beneath bibs in anticipation of peek-a-boo. Independently touching and exploring the world, she is constantly learning so much. The sheer thrill of recognising both herself in photos and family live on Skype.

Double Greeting

Jemima pushes and pulls her hands together and apart. This early, silent clapping is next week replaced by sound as her hands use more force across a greater distance. Baby talk has also taken on more intensity, variety and loudness.

She continues to greet all who encounter her, charming others with her royal wave. She generates such a reaction from her warm friendliness, that now she has created her own style of a double handed wave. Even strangers reciprocate with a two handed salute. The resulting exchange of waves gives both parties incredible joy.

PURE BABY PEARL
TEETHING TIME

The dribble and the niggles. The red patched chin and pale swollen gums. The fingers in the mouth. Oh the troublesome nights of teething. Inconsolable baby. I nurse Jemima back to sleep through the frantic wake ups. I apply the homeopathic *Chamomilla* in every form; the gel, the granules and the pills. I offer cool cucumber strips to suck on by day. Next time I will also assess clove oil concoctions and amber teething necklaces as aids at teething time.

PURE BABY

MONTH 9
DINING
DIRECTIONS

Weaning Progresses

The duties of a doting mum escalate. Somehow I manage to progress with weaning and get out of the house. I am preparing meals, serving baby and myself, clearing up and doing the milk feeds. When each meal outlasts an hour at this early stage of eating, meeting baby's needs indeed encapsulates the entire day.

It's the first supper that Jemima enjoys. Her head plunges forwards with hands clapping. She was hungry and I realise hunger is the best prelude to an easily delivered meal. Then she drinks from a cup just like a cat drains her bowl.

Jemima relished her meals again today. Oh the satisfaction from a baby devouring her food. For breakfast she snapped up my *Oat Temptation* porridge within her fingers. A sticky, messy affair.

Lunch she wolfed down the freshly prepared puree of squash, onion, courgette, broccoli and watercress, accompanied by pureed rice and tiny pieces of *Tofu Joy*.

Then she sang, ate and explored finger foods of maize and rice fusilli, and trees of broccoli and cauliflower. For dinner she enjoyed a similar story, with a few flakes of hake too.

I love seeing how food is really fuelling energy. Upon eating, quiet moaning is quickly replaced by song and laughter, talking and waving.

Jemima enjoys drinking the milk from my whole grain cocktails. I am making combinations with rice, barley and sweet rice. I retrieve the milk and stir the tender grains through a sieve to achieve a very nourishing soft creamy base. Then I add a mixed vegetable puree and occasionally apply my *Sesame Seed Sprinkle* for bonus calcium. I also prepare quinoa flakes cooked with plenty of water, per my recipe *Love Quinoa Two Ways*.

Freshly Cooked Only

As nine months approaches, Jemima's appetite develops and she is generally enjoying three good meals a day. The rhythm of our day develops, and naps after breakfast and lunch fall into a routine.

She loves dining with others at the table, both babies and adults alike. She becomes familiar with protein now, beaming with butterbeans and practicing her pincer grip with plenty of peas.

She knows hot from cold food, refusing cold and devouring warm. She shows her preference for fresh homemade meals, by declining store bought baby food and my few day old purees!

MONTH 9: DINING DIRECTIONS

Sleep In Progress

I notice for the first time Jemima looking tired. Her eyes, which previously remained readily alert, have a weary air. I, too, am absolutely longing for longer sleep at night.

A surprise stretch of five hours the other evening left me feeling liberated the following day. It was as if I had three days worth of fresh energy, and I could touch pre-baby normality from long ago. That day, I went to a late morning yoga class, baby free, thank you grandma!

I praised *Elizabeth Pantley's No Cry Sleep Solution* since my baby had slept for two stretches of five hours. This new feat encouraged me to stick with such a method. *Pantley's* gentle approach is a good fit for baby and I, and had that night enabled better sleep, totally tear free.

Yogi Baby

The yogi baby is exhibiting all manner of fantastic twist and hip openers, planks and downward dogs. She is rotating round in circles like a puppy chasing her tail. Jemima's arms spray in the air on the approach to a children's playground and on arrival at the swings, legs kick frantically from side to side.

Jemima prepares for crawling. She is sliding on the floor, propelling backwards and forwards. Today, I caught her in the kneeling position. On all fours, she is elevating her bottom above ground and rocking her body. She spent nine months evolving under water in the womb. And now she will be making the great transition to a mobile lifestyle, mimicking the ancient amphibia as they crawled out of the sea on all fours.

Ducks In The Bath

She knows my favourite nursery rhymes now and appears to hum along and clap at all the appropriate parts. Ducks are quite simply a love affair. The mere sight of a bright yellow plastic duck heralds the most excitement Jemima can offer.

Ello as Jemima meets her baby friend in a ball pool, well it sounded like that. A definite cry as if to say *remove me now* from the bath in which she had slipped in last night.

I marvel at the manifestation of memory. Experiences are already remembered, recalled and expressed.

PURE BABY PEARL
BABY FOOD QUALITIES

The marathon of activity my baby undertakes daily and the energy that facilitates her Olympic relays is mammoth. Babies present a tiny powerhouse of robust, yang energy, and their development and weight gain are accentuated by soft, yin nourishment. The gentle, fluid and sweet quality of milk supports rapid growth and expansion. Likewise, first foods are sweet and tender, and I offer plenty of soups propelling growth outwards, which feels fitting.

That salt is reserved for the second year is widely recognised. Not only can the kidneys of little ones not tolerate salt, but also salt carries this extremely yang contractive resonance. When babies are programmed to expand and grow into their next sized clothes so quickly, salt can restrict such growth and exert a tightening hold.

For evening meals especially, I strive to use gentle ingredients and relaxing food. Fish, crackers and other heavier foods I reserve for earlier in the day. Anything to encourage sleep!

PURE BABY

MONTH 10
SILENT MOVIE STAR

New Gestures

The super enthusiastic double handed waving continues to befriend everyone. Jemima now greets animals and even insects with her famous wave. As pointing takes hold, she invents a new gesture; the pointed wave. She begins to point in books and towards things she likes and recognises. I am well pleased when her first use of sign language surfaces. Although a rarity, she certainly performs the hand sign for milk at the appropriate moments.

Sleep Patterns

Sleep is still in progress and disturbs me greatly this month. The night-time wake ups were routine and frequent for a week. I make a commitment to teach baby to fall asleep herself and remain asleep. I draw up a chart to monitor all things sleep related.

Then the hot weather sets in and the established last feed of the day left Jemima most awake. For two nights I succumbed to popular sleep training thinking and left my baby sobbing. This futile exercise which lasted only minutes, clouded the rest of my evening. In my anguish, I realised again that I must be flexible, discriminate her cries and only follow what feels right for baby and me.

Change is taking place. New sleep associations have been introduced. Two wake ups a night is now the average and some longer sleep durations have indeed ensued. We decide to try more often with daddy resettling Jemima. I record the daytime naps and intervene to encourage Jemima to enter another sleep cycle.

On The Move

I read that interrupted sleep patterns can accompany developmental leaps. Only a few days short of ten months old, Jemima starts crawling properly. Overnight she is moving with ease as if she had always crawled. Now bags and shoes and table legs are encountered and nearly eaten. On shiny floors she still intently travels by sliding, much like a soldier scurries glued to the ground.

Food, Glorious Food

The two front lower teeth pierce through the gums, pain free, and Jemima's appetite noticeably develops. She *Loves Quinoa* and is enjoying spaghetti, soups with mixed vegetables and my *Soup of Red Lentil & Squash*. She grabs nutritious finger foods including *Tempeh Delight*, steamed kohl rabi and broccoli.

I try to keep up with her self feeding as I remove the outer shell from chickpeas, peas and broad beans, and she gobbles them up. Well cooked millet with cauliflower she also goes for from my *Wholesome Millet Menu*. Steamed courgette pieces she hoovers and raw cucumber too in the hot weather is very welcome.

Infact, I feel very fortunate that Jemima is enjoying eating and so keen to embrace new foods. Lemon scented water she finds odd to start with, but still continues drinking. Nori seaweed snacks serve as great edible paper treats; she grabs these out of my hands and tears them with her teeth. My *Healthy Jelly Glory*, free from sugar and gelatine, she sucks up from her tray with great glee.

Outings

She shows no discomfort by the crazy hot weather, rather she is enjoying the many opportunities for paddling pool activity and outdoor baths. Visits to the children's' playgrounds are excitedly anticipated on the approach, more so than venturing on the swings themselves. She is hugely animated by ducks and dogs, spotting them from afar, waving, pointing and sounding their name.

Silent Movie

Jemima is dancing now. She rocks her body side to side with familiar tunes, and on all fours she sways. She likes giving me objects, kisses too.
Today I jolt when Jemima lifts her foot in readiness to receive her sock, and again when she laughs and points to keys as I take the wrong set. She understands far more than I realise. I must keep explaining and talking to her, well before this silent movie star erupts with language.

PURE BABY PEARL
STRATEGIC SLEEP

I consolidate our bedtime routine.

I make a photo book depicting Jemima's evening rhythm from bathing to reading and sleeping.   I stick flaps over the photos and install our personalised book in the bathroom. As the water fills the bath, Jemima points to her story and then progresses through the pages, smiling at herself.

Over the next few weeks a remarkable shift takes place. The former evening growl and mid-massage yearning for milk is replaced by a relaxed trust in our consistent ritual and the safe knowledge that she will be fed before bed.

The lighting is dim nowadays and blackout curtains avoid any bedtime distraction. Voices are quiet as sleep time approaches.

MONTH 10: SILENT MOVIE STAR

We enjoy the same two beautiful bedtime reads each night. Jemima points to the books in anticipation of their entry to our consistent routine. The soft bunny we introduced not long ago joins Jemima's stories and her slumber.

PURE BABY

MONTH 11
SLEEPY HEAD

Deprived Of Sleep

I am tormented by lack of sleep. I long for sleep and when an opportunity arises, I reawaken quickly or struggle in insomniac fashion. My most basic need for rest is not met and I am a broken person.

I realise this days before my tooth infection takes pace. Then I am forced to rest, permitted to take the time out I need. It feels a similar story to my earlier episodes of mastitis. When will I learn to prioritise the care of myself and bypass a tipping point?

For a week or more the days and nights are difficult. By day my reduced energy levels rub off on baby and she niggles and moans. By night I wail out with the pain of wisdom tooth troubles. I dose up on Chinese herbs and homeopathic remedies but finally I resort to antibiotics. I dose Jemima up on rice milk, express my own milk and hand over baby.

I feel redundant. I am hardly caring for my baby during the day and I am barely breastfeeding her. Expressing is saddening me. My initial idea was to exploit these days and stop feeding baby, but this no longer feels right. I miss the breast feeding massively and tearfully resume the feeds.

Next week Jemima returns to folding her fingers in the sign for milk. I melt at the simplicity and beauty of baby performing such a gesture and silently asking for her sustenance.

Embracing Sleep

My head is heavy and clouded by a string of different sleep approaches. I am at a loose end, unsure of which strategy to go for. I know the inconsistency around bed time is hopeless. Over the next few nights I successfully replace the pre sleep protest with a more gentle wind down in bed. Perhaps the routine is becoming more obvious to baby as she points to the book in anticipation of the coming story.

At last, a night without wake ups, save for a little midnight resettle! Now I see where I had been hindering sleep. I had expected to place Jemima in her cot and for her to sleep just like that!

Of course, Jemima has other ideas. She dislikes sleep, far preferring to be awake and play. Bed and nap times need to be enticing, friendly and baby sensitive. So we say goodbye to all the animals and birds when rest time lingers, since these creatures also prepare for sleep.

MONTH 11: SLEEPY HEAD

Nourishing Sleep

In my sleep deprived state and low energy lethargy, I see that I am in urgent need of some attention. I have attended to my baby's every cry and nappy change, every hour of the day.

Now my kidneys, my body's strong energy source in pre-baby days, are crying out for care. The organs of the kidneys house the vital chi or energy in the body according to the eastern mystics. The kidneys are nourished by sleep at night and my frequent evening awakenings and outdated adrenal alert are greatly disturbing my strength.

I vow to nourish myself better. I commit to twice weekly yoga and take a gap from teaching public cooking classes.

Digestion Develops

Jemima dines on her highchair throne. If I have the opportunity to prepare, a small portion buffet awaits. She rigorously points to that which she likes or wants more of. She tells me of her hunger with a burst of short vowel sounds. Often I yoyo up and down in search of more food to keep up with her noisy appetite. *Tofu Joy* has become a favourite, chickpeas too and of course nori strips. A macrobiotic baby no less!

She sucks up ribbons of Chinese and pointed cabbage. She laps up a light miso broth from my *Mini Miso Soup* and loves foraging for bready croutons in her soups. Noodles and sauce too are hoovered up in a messy foray. She seems pleased with plaice and points for more.

Now I am beginning to share food with baby and cook dishes that we all can enjoy. I start an early version of a *First Stir Fry*. I prepare vegetables with a little oil and cook them in a heavy covered pan for a time so that they tenderise in their own juices. Steamed vegetables had been taking a long time to soften, as if all the nutrition was lost in the steaming water.

From her nappies, I know Jemima's digestive system is suddenly more developed. Food is being much better broken down and absorbed. Her bold appetite has certainly escalated with her progression in movement.

Foot Ball

Playing ball is still Jemima's top pastime. The mere sight of any ball like object sends excited legs and arms a waving. She catches and returns balls in great, young relays. She throws the ball from over head and takes several balls on journeys across the room or lawn. She happily initiates ball games with adults and babies alike.

Crawling is gathering momentum. The pace quickens and the distance of travel widens. Jemima, with curiosity, pulls herself to standing and is beginning to use her feet to balance upon. These little feet which thus far have served no great purpose, are now starting to flatten and spread over the floor and support her weight for just an instant.

PURE BABY PEARL
SPIRIT OF SURRENDER

I relax, resign to bedtime, however long it takes. Previously I am anxious, worried and tightening my body. I have been tiptoeing on edge and holding my breath. All I had wanted was to escape baby's bedroom as fast as I could. My yang energy has been ruining the soft, relaxing atmosphere our nightly routine was intended to create.

I have witnessed how my energy is directly picked up by baby. Through my days of fatigue, Jemima's spirit has plunged and over the moments in presence, her energy has soared. In the company of little ones especially, any other agenda may not be considered.

I soften and surrender to my little being who melts my heart and engulfs me with love. I yield to her beauty, innocence and faith in life. With a mother's love I try to let go of the demands of the day, and join Jemima with gentle tenderness.

PURE BABY

MONTH 12
PURE PERCEPTION

Daily Gift

Every day I receive a token flower, a Lego tulip picked out from a box of endless shapes and features. A gift from my baby. She is offering me her food and drinks now too. The first sense of sharing impresses upon her. She plants affectionate kisses on other babies, and continues reaching out in communication with her loyal, royal wave.

Dancing In The Sky

She laughs hysterically when initiating games of peek-a-boo, teasing my involvement and response. Rough and tumble she loves, dancing she enjoys and playing is the best. Books she locates promptly, turning the pages from cover to cover. She is learning fast now and mimicking others at the scene. Towers of bricks are beginning to mount and then toppling, crayons are first etching marks on paper and then moving to the mouth, and stairs are a climbing!

I am alerted to every bird and plane that arches through the sky. Her perception is perfect, the senses so acute. Even the highest aircraft or spec in flight does not go unnoticed. She forms the same sign to tell me of her sighting. The sign for milk she uses widely and leaves me to decipher the meaning.

First Words

Her two front, upper teeth have dropped down through her gums. She notices her mouth structure change and now relishes biting into food and clicking her tongue on her palate. A tapestry of sound like words emerge each day. Intonations of *dog*, *dirty* and *daddy* then *mama* and exclamations of *look* and *bye-bye* weave from within. These intuitive noises arise naturally in the most appropriate situation, and each word is voiced just once on a single day alone.

Delight is squealed on recognising images of babies or her familiar toys, food and plastic balls. Still Jemima takes her time to get comfortable in some new situations. Once she is relaxed, babbles of talking bubble. She is curious about unusual surroundings, sensing the energy people emit straight away. She warms to most, and withdraws from few.

Sleep we still tackle. I know we are on the cusp of sleeping through, when simply a stroke is needed during the night. Next week as words gather pace and a growth spurt hits, sleep regresses and screams ensue.

MONTH 12: PURE PERCEPTION

Sleepy Intentions

The plot thickens. The seasons change and evenings are getting darker earlier. Suddenly lengthy bedtimes and night awakenings are replaced by easy slumber and full sleep stretches. I am overjoyed. I have been praying for continued peaceful sleep for us all.

Tactics change and dinner now preludes bath time. Previously this meal took place too early. No wonder Jemima awoke in the wee morning hours hungry. Now we assume a good rhythm of naps and snacks, playing and dining.

I decipher the time that suits baby best for bed and stick to this. We play in the cot by day and consolidate our routine by night. Stroking and patting is replaced by long sshing sounds and repetitions of our sleepy mantra.

Just days ahead of her first birthday, Jemima sleeps through the night and entertains good naps during the day.

My greatest challenge by far this year has been sleep. Leading baby to sleep through, allowing myself to rest and carrying on amidst the haze of sleep deprivation.

I have bemoaned the wasted time and effort these sleep trials have entailed. I have longed for successive hours of rest. I have walked endless circuits and endured hours knelt over the cot. I have fed and stroked, rocked and ssshed. I have always responded to my baby's pleas, been present to her learning.

Some may say I have been too fast to respond or remained too close. But I have done what felt right, what felt good to my heart and loyal to my child. My mind battled for weeks between the gentle sleep strategies which still involved crying, and living with disruptive sleep.

In my mind I heard the loud calls of rest for us all. I knew of the urgent requirement for solid sleep for a growing baby and of the fundamental need for rest for a parent, wife and worker. Nevertheless, I attended to my baby by day, explaining and playing. Why should I act differently by night and ignore my baby's moans for a simple touch?

Babies are quick learners and I did want to foster good sleep habits. My mothering was suffering. Infact my whole being was anguished by less than optimal sleep. I entered into a gentle sleep plan of the gradual retreat variety. I prayed and visualised, wrote aims and made intentions. I asked for help from all the unseen beings, that they may stroke my little ones' eyelids to sleep and help her entry to the land of nod.

On the very first evening of our plan, my little one fell asleep with ease and remained asleep all night! I salute the power of intention, coupled with Jemima's readiness for such a plan.

Milk & Meals

I introduce Jemima to the kitchen and talk through the cooking as if giving a demonstration. She takes an interest, reaching out to touch the vegetables I am preparing. She smells the

94

seasonings and listens to the pressure cooker. In her highchair she claps her hands with pleasure and offers me her favourite foods.

After eating she is keen on cleaning her tray, and copies the way I use a sponge. I see that she loves to do things by herself and my praise and recognition of this brings smiles and pride to her face. Oh the rate of learning is so rapid.

As the final weeks of the year draw closer, I realise the breastfeeds have naturally declined. Yesterday I only fed Jemima once. Only two months ago, four feeds were the norm. Baby has led the way. Well, she is devouring her breakfast, lunch and dinner, going for seconds and saying yes to every new food offering. Indeed I am very happy with her openness to food, her appetite and her joyful eating.

Breakfast

For breakfast she goes for *Oat Temptation* porridge with cinnamon, cooked apple or *Sesame Seed Sprinkle*. Tender millet with sweet potato is another early meal she enjoys. We share the same food now. I either remove portions for Jemima and then season the rest, or reserve any seasoning for later.

Hors D'Oeuvre

I make soups with onion, carrot, courgette and wakame sea vegetable and she drinks the nutritious broth. The soup contents make for ideal and easily prepared finger foods. Yesterdays soup ingredients of peas, leeks, sweet potato and rice noodles she lapped up from her tray.

Jemima continues to love a creamy *Soup of Sweet Potato, Carrot & Coconut* and my *Soup Of Red Lentil & Squash*. She gulps down these thick blended dishes without hesitation.

Mochi croutons are a treat which Jemima likes to chew. These pounded sweet rice cubes are a nourishing delicacy which I fry or simply add to soups.

What's For Dinner?

Meals are detected, ingredients surveyed and praised. Jemima goes for the new food options first when presented her dinner plate. Even after dessert is devoured, a new style tofu portion, misjudged and ending on the floor, is happily located.

Jemima is belonging to our bumper season of blackberries, tomatoes and pears. She yearns after such produce as she views us picking the fruits of our garden.

Plenty of finger foods allow me to step back at meal times, letting Jemima feed herself. She even wishes to use the spoon on her own. I place full teaspoons on her tray and she directs spoon to mouth with great pleasure.

She reaches out for what I am eating. Rye bread and oat cakes she nibbles. Morsels of white fish and occasional salmon she really enjoys. She really loves a *Tofu Scramble* or a stew of red lentils and vegetables. I offer her clumps of oatmeal, lentil paté, tempeh blocks or sticky millet and quinoa grains.

First Cookies

For afters, she likes an amasake pudding. This yummy sweet treat I prepare with rice cream and amasake, the nourishing fermented rice custard treat. Once I made the amasake with kuzu, the healing plant thickener, and Jemima devoured several servings. She also enjoys cooked apple and berries. Banana and avocado she still relishes raw.

I make her *First Oat Cookies*. I combine cooked jumbo oats from breakfast with ground almonds, a sprinkle of ginger powder and few squeezes of rice syrup. I prepare a baking tray of these biscuits and admire the resulting flour free cookies. Baked flour goods are heavy on the digestion and can be mucus forming. Jemima likes the outcome too, and enjoys my cooked oat cookies as snacks and after meals.

À La Carte

As the first year closes, we all celebrate with a Jemima timed dinner in a fine restaurant. We forget that pristine white tablecloths adorn the tables and noise levels are at a minimum. Nevertheless, Jemima joins us at the table. At home with the atmosphere, she charms the waiters, shares in our meal and keeps her area spotless.

From across the table, she places her hand to mouth, followed by extending her arm. She blew me a kiss! Thank you my precious one, my child, a baby no more.

PURE BABY PEARL
POWER THROUGH LIFE

My baby's bursts of activity all began with excited kicking of the legs in the early weeks. This outpouring of energy travelled up her spine, adding strength to her muscles to first lift her head independently, and then support a seated posture by month six. After the coordination of crawling emerged, this silent and powerful energy pulled her to a standing position.

The ancient eastern medics termed this energy our life force and housed it in the kidneys. They plotted the movement of the energy in a meridian from the feet up the body. Now I see the sheer importance of kidney strength in giving power to the body, and how this energy propels baby's development.

Baby's constitution and inherited energy are connected to her kidneys. Thus far, my condition and experience of pregnancy, birth and nursing have impacted on baby's disposition and played with her nature. Over the first year, I feel her constitution is still a little pliable. I have upheld Jemima's kidney strength by nourishing her health and safeguarding her exposure to toxicity.

MONTH 12: PURE PERCEPTION

May my early investment cement baby's foundations for robust health, and frame her constitution for a lifetime.

PURE BABY

THE FIRST FINISH

As this tremendous first year of motherhood draws to a close, I reflect on the precious time and my nurturing of a new life. How will I hold the memories of my young baby when the weeks have whizzed by and our daily encounters together have blurred the edges of her growth? I can no longer recall how she was at ten days, two months or even last week.

I know I will remember her eyes. The long, unashamed eye contact from so early in life. Her longing to look straight into my eyes and spread her face with smile.

I will recall carrying her close in the baby carrier, her head itching to see the world, until sleep overtakes and she rests her cosy self upon me.

The friendly greeting of her two little hands waving is marked in my mind. The wave has been her silent communication and symbol of recognition. She has extended waves in love and without judgement to all people, animals and birds.

I will remember her quick awareness and attunement to nature. Her noticing the sunlight and the shadows, the birds and the bees, all long before me.

I imagine the memory of the enormous physical demand on my body will diminish. The constant lifting and moving, forever up and down, the feeding and the rocking. The drain of being on permanent high alert to baby's sounds.

The planning to go upstairs, the preparation to leave the house and the strain to arrive on time. The wild mess of weaning. The focused blitz a thirty five minute nap brings, the frustration at not being able to complete a thing and the sheer sleep deprivation.

Welcoming baby has indeed been all consuming, meeting her needs and facilitating her happiness.

Yet, nurturing Jemima has revealed a world of love. She has melted my heart and brought my full attention to the moment.

She has taught me so much about living in true health. Her limitless energy, playful fun, and spirited sounds. Her appetite for food, life and friendships. Her thirst for learning, wonder and oneness with all. Her joy and intuition.

As the first year closes, I step back and watch Jemima upright now, with her honest vigour for life, her complete beauty and joyful presence. I thank all the forces for blessing me with this child.

PURE BABY
COOKBOOK

The cookbook of essential, wholesome dishes for expectant and new mums and weaning babies follows. Recipes use only honestly healthy, natural ingredients, and there are few instructions to enable ease and speed of creation.

Cultivate your baby's appetite and support their discovery of food, rapid growth and digestive development. The dishes for baby from *Month 6: First Foods* onwards form a pure and healthy weaning programme. These recipes accompany the former diaries to provide a gradually expanding repertoire of menus for your baby to enjoy.

Recipes for mum serve four generous portions, and those for baby include modifications for all the family to sample.

Measurements are an indicated guide and variations on the recipes are comprised, to allow for your freedom in the kitchen.

PURE BABY

PREGNANCY RECIPES

MISO MINESTRONE

A hearty and delicious one pot soup rich in goodness from an array of vegetables and nourishing butterbeans. Vitalising miso adds a flavourful twist and offers the benefits of gut friendly bacteria. Read more on the marvels of miso in the *Mini Miso Soup*. Perhaps now, amidst the fatigue of the first trimester, a friend or partner can create this uplifting meal for you.

Ingredients:
1 onion diced
1 clove garlic finely cut
2 carrots cut in small pieces
1 courgette cut in small pieces
1 strip wakame sea vegetable
1 - 2 cups cooked butterbeans
1 cup tinned tomatoes
Water
Dash sesame oil
Half teaspoon sea salt
1 teaspoon dried Italian herbs
2 tablespoons brown rice or barley miso paste
1 tablespoon fresh basil finely cut

Preparation:

Heat the sesame oil and sauté the onions and garlic with a pinch of salt for a few minutes. Then add the carrot and courgette. Rinse the wakame sea vegetable and cut it into centimetre long pieces. Add beans, tinned tomatoes, dry herbs and water to fill the pan. Bring to the boil. Cover and reduce the heat and simmer for 15 minutes. Add sea salt and cook for a further few minutes. Dilute miso in a little cooking liquid and add to the soup. Simmer for another few minutes.
Garnish with fresh basil.

SPEEDY SALT & VINEGAR GREENS

Ditch the crisps and switch to this perfectly healthy snack or side dish with regularity throughout your pregnancy.

Ingredients:

1 bunch leafy green vegetables such as kale, spring greens, cavelo nero, chard, spinach
Dash sesame oil
Sprinkle shoyu or tamari soy sauce
Sprinkle brown rice vinegar
Pinch sea salt
2 teaspoons sesame seeds

Preparation:

Remove the tough stem from kale, spring greens or chard. Slice the leafy greens very finely. Heat the oil in a pan. Add the greens and a pinch of salt. Fry for a few minutes. Then add a sprinkle of shoyu and rice vinegar to taste. Garnish with sesame seeds.

QUICK LEMON SCENTED QUINOA SALAD

A favourite fresh, zesty dish. Fabulous quinoa and pumpkin seeds will nourish your blood in pregnancy with essential protein, iron and more.

Ingredients:

1 cup quinoa
2 cups water
Zest from one lemon
Juice from half a lemon
Handful pumpkin seeds
1 spring onion finely cut
Pinch sea salt
Dash shoyu or tamari soy sauce

Preparation:

Place the quinoa in a pan and add water and lemon juice. Bring to the boil, then reduce the heat, cover the pan and simmer for 15 minutes, until tender. Transfer to a serving bowl and add a

107

dash of shoyu or tamari, and fold in lemon zest, pumpkin seeds and spring onion.

Enjoy with *Gentle Lentil Dahl*.

GENTLE LENTIL DAHL

An easily prepared dish with nutritious lentils and gentle fragrances. A plant protein staple in pregnancy.

Ingredients:

1 onion finely sliced
1 inch piece ginger root peeled and finely cut
2 cloves garlic finely cut
2 carrots cut in small pieces
3 strips celery cut in small pieces
1 cup green or brown lentils
2 cups water
1 inch strip kombu sea vegetable
Dash sesame oil
Pinch cumin seeds
Pinch turmeric
Sea salt
Handful fresh coriander finely cut

Preparation:

Rinse the lentils and place them in a pan with 2 cups water and kombu sea vegetable. Bring to the boil, then reduce the heat, cover and simmer for 30 minutes until the lentils are soft.

Meanwhile, heat the oil in another pan and sauté the onion with a pinch of sea salt. Add the garlic and ginger, and then fold in the carrot and celery with a teaspoon of sea salt. Add the cumin seeds and turmeric, cover and cook for 8 minutes, stirring occasionally.

When the lentils are cooked, combine in the pan with the vegetables and add a pinch of sea salt. Cook for a further minute, sample and add any more salt to taste. Garnish with fresh coriander.

Serve with *Quick Lemon Scented Quinoa or* brown basmati rice and blanched broccoli.

SECRET TEMPEH STIR FRY

Embrace the secret ingredient of tempeh in pregnancy and receive ample nutritious benefits. Tempeh is revered for its nourishing properties, and high protein and B vitamin content. Sauerkraut and alfalfa sprouts also provide rich nutrition and require virtually no preparation. Here we play with a host of flavours in the marinade; salty shoyu, sweet apple juice, sour sauerkraut and pungent ginger.

Ingredients:

1 block tempeh
1 inch piece ginger root peeled and finely cut
1 onion
5 small mushrooms

3 handfuls alfalfa sprouts
3 tablespoons sauerkraut
1 inch strip kombu sea vegetable
3 tablespoons shoyu or tamari soy sauce
1 cup apple juice or 3 tablespoons apple juice concentrate
Bay leaf
Sesame oil

Preparation:

Tempeh is often purchased frozen. If this is the case, allow to defrost then cut inch wide cubes. Place the kombu strip in a pan with the ginger, tempeh cubes and bay leaf. Top with shoyu, apple juice concentrate and water to cover. Bring the marinade to the boil and then reduce the heat and simmer for 15 minutes.

Meanwhile finely slice the onion and mushrooms. Once the tempeh is cooked, heat 4 tablespoons oil in a frying pan. Now fry the tempeh pieces for a few minutes on each side until golden in colour. Set the tempeh aside. Then fry the onions in the oil with a pinch of sea salt for a few minutes. Add the mushrooms and fry for a further few minutes. Add the alfalfa, a dash of the tempeh marinade and return the fried tempeh to the pan.

Serve and enjoy accompanied by any cooked grain or noodles. Use the remaining yummy marinade as a stock for a parents-only soup such as the *Surprise In A Soup* or *Minestrone Miso Soup*.

COSY FRUIT PLATE

A warm fruit ensemble melting with natural fruit sugars. This recipe also uses rice syrup, a sugar-free kitchen prerequisite in pregnancy.

Ingredients:
2 pears
2 apples
Handful raisins
1 tablespoon lemon zest
3 tablespoons rice syrup
Drop vanilla extract
Water

Preparation:
Place the raisins in a small bowl and cover with hot water. Let soak for 10 minutes. Cut the apple and pear into small pieces, no need to peel the fruit first. Then place all the ingredients together in a pan. Bring to the boil, then cover and reduce the heat and simmer for 8 minutes. Enjoy!

PURE BABY

NEW MUM'S MEALS

SURPRISE IN A SOUP

One pan, one moment, one hungry mummy to feed. This is your dish. A strengthening and complete meal in itself. Hearty veggies, noodles and fish infused with rich flavours will nourish any new mother.

Ingredients:

1 onion finely cut
2 carrots cut in small chunks
1 courgette cut in small chunks
Third butternut squash or pumpkin cut in small chunks
Dash sesame oil
1 serving udon noodles
Fillet of fish such as hake, cod, salmon or haddock with skin removed
1 strip wakame sea vegetable rinsed and cut into small strips
Water
4 dashes ume vinegar
1-2 tablespoons bouillon
2 dashes shoyu or tamari soy sauce
Handful watercress leaves, with stems removed

PURE BABY

Preparation:

Cook the noodles according to the instructions on the packet. Discard water and set the noodles aside in a bowl of cold water to prevent sticking. Now heat a dash of oil in the pan and add the sliced onions. Cover and cook for 4 minutes. Then add the carrot, courgette and squash and wakame sea vegetable. Add water to more than cover, and bring to the boil. Cover and reduce the heat and simmer for 15 minutes. Add bouillon, ume vinegar and fish. Allow the fish to cook in the yummy broth, by simmering for a further 5 minutes. Add shoyu, cooked noodles, adjust flavours to taste and serve garnished with watercress.

Variations:

Enjoy the recipe by adding cooked buckwheat or barley instead of noodles, and fried tofu or tempeh in place of fish. For deep rich flavours, introduce a hint of ginger juice and miso in the last few minutes of the cooking time.

NEW MUM'S CONGEE DELUXE

A rich, warming dish, which cultivates the energy following childbirth, and nourishes a fine quality of breast milk. The bonus ingredient is sweet rice; known as *mochi*, and this adds further strength to your milk. This dish is perfect for new mothers and ideal to enjoy at breakfast or any other time of day.

NEW MUM'S MEALS

Ingredients:

1 cup whole grains (eg. half cup short grain brown rice and half cup sweet mochi rice)
3 cups water
1 cup sweet vegetables such as carrot, squash, onion or pumpkin, cut into small chunks
2 tablespoons brown rice or barley miso paste
Pinch sea salt
Handful sunflower or pumpkin seeds
Pressure cooker or heavy pan with a lid

Preparation:

Select a cup of whole grains from brown rice, barley, sweet rice and whole oat groats. Choose one grain alone, or make a lovely combination of 2 or 3 different varieties.

Rinse the grains and place in the pan. Add the small vegetable chunks on top. Then add 3 cups water, a pinch of sea salt, cover with a lid and bring to the boil. If you are using a pressure cooker, bring this up to pressure. Reduce the heat and cook for one hour.

Fold in the miso and serve garnished with sunflower or pumpkin seeds.

MUMMY RICE PUDDING

Fast to prepare and a wholesome treat, my yummy mummy pudding recipe uses the very soft grains leftover from making baby rice milk.

Ingredients:

1 cup cooked grain (grain cooked with at least five times as much water for an hour or more, as per *Baby Rice Milk Recipe*)
Half cup water or coconut milk
1 tablespoon hazelnut butter
3 splashes apple juice concentrate
4 dashes rice syrup

Preparation:

Combine all the ingredients in a pan and bring to the boil. Cover and simmer for five minutes. Enjoy!

MONTH 6+

BABY RICE MILK

Homemade rice milk confers all the nutrition of whole grains as an easily digestible drink. Rice milk is most nourishing for baby and can also be enjoyed by all the family. I often use this wonderful tonic to thicken soups and make creamy sauces. Here is baby's first recipe.

Ingredients:

1 cup whole grains (eg. half cup short grain brown rice and half cup sweet mochi rice)
7 cups water
Pressure cooker or heavy pan with a lid
Sieve or food mill

Preparation:

Rinse the grains and place in the pan. Add the water and leave the grains to soak for three hours or overnight. Then put the pan on a medium flame, cover with a lid and bring to the boil. If you are using a pressure cooker, bring this up to pressure. Reduce the heat and cook for one hour to one hour and a half.

Now transfer the contents of the pan to a sieve over a bowl and stir the mixture through the sieve. Alternatively use a food mill here. The resulting extracted liquid is grain milk. This can be stored in the fridge for 3 days.

Variations:

As baby grows, I play with the consistency of the milk in three ways. First, I gradually reduce the amount of water added to the pan with successive weeks. Secondly, I stir the grain through the sieve with some vigour in order to create a nourishing and thick rice cream. Finally, I achieve an array of nutrition and taste by cooking a variety of grains in combination. I use two or three different varieties from selections of brown rice, millet, oat groats, sweet rice, pot barley and more.

MONTH 7+

SOUP OF SWEET POTATO, CARROT & COCONUT

A thick, hearty puree for baby and lovely soup for you.

Ingredients:

1 onion sliced
1 carrot sliced
2 sweet potatoes peeled and cut into small chunks
Water
Coconut cream – optional to use from month 9

Preparation:

Cut the vegetables and place them in a pan. Add water to cover and bring to the boil. Then cover the pan and reduce the heat. Simmer for 15 minutes until the carrots are tender. Blend using a handheld blender and serve.

Variations:

By month 9, once baby is digesting food well, include a little organic coconut cream for extra richness and a tropical scent. Add the coconut in the last few minutes of the cooking time.

Vary the recipe by adding any other sweet vegetables such as parsnip, pumpkin or cauliflower.

MONTH 8+

GREEN BABY SOUP WITH FRESH DILL

A nutritious broth for baby. Enjoy yourself with a hint of miso or bouillon seasoning.

Ingredients:

1 courgette sliced
4 leaves Chinese cabbage sliced
Handful watercress with stalks removed and finely chopped
1 teaspoon fresh dill cut finely
Water

Preparation:

Cut the vegetables and place the courgette and Chinese cabbage in the pan. Add water to cover and bring to the boil. Then cover the pan and reduce the heat. Simmer for 10 minutes, then add the watercress and fresh dill. Cook another 5 minutes. Blend using a handheld blender and serve.

PURE BABY

PURE BABY MENU
MONTH 9+

TOFU JOY

Tofu provides the first introduction to plant proteins since it is so easy to digest. Tender tofu is indeed a firm favourite of my baby. Infact all other children we introduce to tofu, take a great liking to this nutritious soybean food.

Ingredients:

Half block of tofu of medium firmness
Half inch piece of kombu sea vegetable
Water

Preparation:

Cut the tofu into small cubes. Place the kombu, tofu and water to cover in a pan and bring to the boil. Reduce the heat and cover, and simmer for 5 minutes. Give your baby tofu cubes as finger foods or mash together with vegetable or grain purees.

LOVE QUINOA TWO WAYS

I found quinoa a fantastic early food for baby. Soft and easy to digest, nourishing and fast to prepare, quinoa makes a versatile staple. Begin by giving baby the cooked quinoa *flakes*, since the flakes tenderise so easily. Later in the first year, serve *whole* quinoa gently cooked.

Ingredients:

Half cup quinoa flakes
1 cup whole quinoa
Water

Preparation:

For the flakes, place flakes in the pan with 2 cups water. Bring to the boil, then reduce the heat, cover and simmer for 15 minutes, until tender.

For the whole grain, place 1 cup in the pan with 3 cups water. Bring to the boil, then reduce the heat, cover and simmer for 20 minutes. Check that the quinoa is tender. Then turn off the heat and let the cooked quinoa sit in the covered pan for a further 6 minutes to further soften.

Baby's cooked quinoa should be very soft and porridge like. Serve with a vegetable puree or make a quinoa pudding with rice syrup and cooked pear.

OAT TEMPTATION

Cooked oats become very soft and easy to digest. Beware a sticky messy baby, when oat clumps become irresistible finger foods.

Ingredients:

1 cup rolled oats
3 cups water
Half apple diced
Half teaspoon rice syrup or barley malt – optional

Preparation:

Place the oats in a pan, with diced fruit and add water. Bring to the boil, then reduce the heat, cover and simmer for 20 minutes until the oats are very soft.

Note: If you use jumbo oats, they require a longer cooking time than rolled oats.

Serve a small portion of oats for baby. Fold in a little barley malt or rice syrup for a sweet porridge.

SESAME SEED SPRINKLE

A perfect way to add calcium and flavour to baby's food. As baby nears the end of the first year, experiment with ground walnuts and almonds, and adding tahini and hazelnut butters to meals for extra richness.

Ingredients:

Half cup sesame seeds
Mortar & pestle, or Japanese version called suribachi

Preparation:

Toast the sesame seeds by heating them in a pan. Keep moving the seeds in the pan for a few minutes until they become a little golden and fragrant. Now grind them with the mortar and pestle or suribachi.

Sprinkle a pinch over baby's porridge and other meals.

MONTH 10+

WHOLESOME MILLET MENU

Millet is a lovely, gluten free whole grain which looks a little like quinoa. Millet takes longer to cook than quinoa, but the resulting warming, nourishing and strengthening dish is well worthwhile.

Ingredients:

1 cup millet
3 ½ cups water
Third cauliflower cut into small florets – optional

Preparation:

Rinse the millet and place in a pan. Add the cauliflower and water and bring to a boil. Cover with a tight lid and reduce the heat. Refrain from stirring while the millet is cooking, otherwise the grain tends to stick to the bottom of the pan. Simmer for 35 minutes until the millet is tender.

Enjoy a millet porridge with baby at breakfast time, and add a sprinkle of cinnamon. Alternatively, serve at lunch or dinner with cooked chickpeas and courgette strips. Offer millet cubes as finger foods, once the millet has cooled and firmed. Or make a millet pudding with fruit pieces and rice syrup or barley malt.

SOUP OF RED LENTIL & SQUASH

A thick and nutritious soup with hidden veggies, plant proteins and sea vegetable goodness. Both you and baby can enjoy this yummy dish.

Ingredients:

Half cup red lentils
1 onion sliced
1 carrot sliced
1 cup butternut squash cut into small chunks
1 inch strip kombu sea vegetable
Water

Preparation:

Rinse the red lentils and cut the vegetables. Place the red lentils in a pan with the kombu, and add the onion, carrot and butternut squash on top. Add water to cover and bring to the boil. Remove any foam that forms with a spoon and then cover the pan with a tight lid and reduce the heat. Simmer for 35 minutes until the lentils are tender. Blend and serve with *Wholesome Millet*, noodles or whole quinoa from *Love Quinoa*.

PURE BABY MENU: MONTH 10+

As baby grows older, I serve this dish as a stew without using the blender. I add fresh herbs such as basil or coriander and cooked noodles to make a hearty meal. Alternatively, I allow the lentils to cool and firm and serve pieces of lentil paté as finger foods.

HEALTHY JELLY GLORY

Baby and I relish this sugar and gelatine-free jelly, especially on midsummer days. She laps up teaspoons of the gel like treat and practices her pincer grip, by picking up slippery fragments from her tray.

Ingredients:

1 cup water
1 cup apple juice
3 tablespoons agar agar flakes
1 tablespoon rice syrup
Half cup seasonal soft fruit such as pear or strawberries

Preparation:

Bring water and apple juice to the boil. Add the rice syrup and agar flakes and simmer until the flakes have dissolved, about 10 minutes. Meanwhile cut the fruit into small pieces and arrange in a serving dish. Pour the hot liquid into the dish and allow to cool and set.

PURE BABY

MONTH 11+

FIRST STIR FRY

Sesame oil adds richness and is a good balanced oil, stable at high temperatures. I select baby friendly vegetables; non-fibrous, tender, and easy to digest.

Ingredients:

1 onion
1 courgette
1 sweet potato
4 leaves Chinese cabbage
Sesame oil
Wok

Preparation:

Heat a dash of oil in the wok. Finely slice or even grate the vegetables. First add the onion and cook for a few minutes, stirring frequently. Then add the other vegetables and continue stir frying until the vegetables are very tender.

MINI MISO SOUP FOR MUM TOO

Miso makes a nutritious tonic for vitality and strength, good digestive functioning and full body health. Miso paste contains living enzymes and friendly bacteria that are most beneficial to the gut. Since miso carries a salty flavour, be sure to go very mild for baby.

Ingredients:

Half onion
Half courgette
Few leaves Chinese cabbage
Any other non-fibrous vegetables such as sweet potato, butternut squash, cauliflower, broccoli
1 inch strip wakame sea vegetable
3 cups water
Brown rice or barley miso paste

Preparation:

Bring water to the boil in a pan and finely slice the vegetables. Add the onions first and cook for 4 minutes before adding the other vegetables and wakame sea vegetable. Bring to the boil, then cover the pan and simmer for ten minutes, until the vegetables are tender.

Place a ladle of broth in baby's cup or bowl and mix in less than a fifth teaspoon of miso. Offer the cooked vegetables as finger foods.

For yourself, allow roughly 1 teaspoon of miso per serving, and adjust to your taste.

Note: if you are making a batch of soup to last a few days, only add the miso paste to your stock when you are about to enjoy the soup. This is because the miso contains active ingredients that are denatured at high temperatures.

PURE BABY

MONTH 12+

TOFU SCRAMBLE

A super scrambled tofu dish using a little oil and fast cooking vegetable slithers. Add a pinch of salt or shoyu and serve for the rest of the family.

Ingredients:

1 block tofu
1 courgette grated
Third butternut squash or 1 sweet potato peeled and grated
Dash sesame oil
Fresh basil – optional

Preparation:

Grate the vegetables and then crumble the tofu between your fingers. Heat the oil in a pan and add the courgette. Fry for a minute, then add the squash or sweet potato, followed by the crumbled tofu. Cook for five minutes and add fresh herbs in the last minute.

TEMPEH DELIGHT

Tempeh is incredibly nourishing and satisfying, and is more substantial than tofu. In addition to being protein rich, tempeh also carries the health benefits of the fermented soy bean.

Ingredients:

1 block of tempeh
Half inch piece of kombu sea vegetable
Water

Preparation:

Tempeh is often purchased frozen. If this is the case, allow to defrost then cut into inch long pieces. Place the kombu, tempeh and water to cover in a pan and bring to the boil. Reduce the heat and cover, and simmer for 15 minutes. Give your baby the tempeh pieces as finger foods or serve together with vegetable and grain dishes.

Variations:

After cooking the tempeh in this way, you can fry the pieces and make a tempeh sandwich with vegan mayonnaise and natural ketchup for yourself. Alternatively, bake the tempeh in a yummy marinade with flavours such as garlic, tamari soy sauce and orange juice or enjoy my *Secret Tempeh Stir Fry*, located in the *Pregnancy Recipes*.

FIRST OAT COOKIES

My recipe is gentle on baby's young digestive system. I use oats that have already been cooked, instead of raw oat flakes or flour. Cooked oats are easier to assimilate than raw flakes, and baked flour products can be very mucus-forming and heavy on the digestive system.

Ingredients:

1 cup cooked jumbo or rolled oats
Pinch ginger powder
2 tablespoons ground almonds
3 tablespoons rice syrup

Preparation:

Combine the ingredients and heat the oven to 180°C. Prepare a baking tray with oiled baking parchment. Place spoonfuls of the mixture on the tray. Bake the cookies for 12 minutes or until the top goes slightly golden. Enjoy!

PURE BABY

MEET MUM

Anna Freedman is expert in taking the mystery out of macrobiotics. Her sensible natural food approach and delicious recipes are widely followed for their health expanding effects, ease to integrate into modern living and wonderful taste.

Anna is a qualified macrobiotic cook and health coach with a biology training, and wide experience teaching, catering and positively changing lives.

She appears on TV and radio and is featured regularly by many publications including *Vegetarian Living* and *Juno* Natural Parenting Magazine.

Anna is founder of *Wholefood Harmony*, the Cookery School which inspires health through delicious natural cuisine.

She lives in London, England with her husband Scott and daughter, Jemima. For further details please visit *www.wholefoodharmony.com* or email *welcome@wholefoodharmony.com*.

PURE BABY

BIBLIOGRAPHY

Gopnik, Alison, Andrew Meltzoff and Patricia Kuhl. *The Scientist In The Crib: What early learning tells us about the mind.* New York: HarperCollins, 2001.

Gordon, Yehudi. *Birth And Beyond: Pregnancy, birth, your baby and family – the definitive guide.* London, England: Random House, 2002.

Karmiloff, Kyra and Annette Karmiloff-Smith. *Everything Your Baby Would Ask if only he or she could talk.* London, England: Carroll & Brown, 2003.

Kushi, Michio, and Aveline Kushi. *Raising Healthy Kids: A book of childcare & natural family health.* New York: Avery Publishing Group, 1994.

McKay, Pinky. *Sleeping Like a Baby: Simple sleep solutions for infants and toddlers.* Australia: Penguin, 2006.

Motha, Gowri and Karen S Macleod. *Gentle Birth Method: The month by month programme.* London, England: Thorsons, 2004.

Pantly, Elizabeth. *The No-Cry Sleep Solution: Gentle ways to help your baby sleep through the night.* New York: McGraw-Hill, 2006.

Sears, William, and Martha Sears. *Baby Book: Everything you need to know about your baby from birth to age two.* London, England: HarperCollins, 2005.

Sunderland, Margot. *What Every Parent Needs To Know: The remarkable effects of love, nurture and play on your child's development.* London, England: DK, 2007.

Verney, Thomas, and Weintraub, Pamela. *Tomorrow's Baby: The art and science of parenting from conception through infancy.* New York: Simon & Schuster, 2002.

Welton, Rebecca. *Baby Sleeping Trust Techniques: Alternatives to controlled crying.* England: Spottiswoode Publishing, 2013.

RESOURCES

Active Birth Centre

www.activebirthcentre.com

Offers active birth programmes with water birth, pregnancy, and professional training.

BabiesKnow

www.babiesknow.com

Encourages healthy, loving and connected relationships at every stage of family life.

Birth Preparation

www.gentlebirthbaby.com

CD - The Jeyarani Way: Prepare for a natural birth with self hypnosis and visualisation.

Birthlight

www.birthlight.com

Promotes an integrated, holistic approach to pregnancy, birth and babyhood, and uses yoga techniques.

Music for Birth

Comfort Zone by Steven Halpern.

Organic Delivery Company

www.organicdeliverycompany.co.uk

High quality organic produce delivered in and around London.

Sea Vegetables
www.seaveg.co.uk
Suppliers of hand picked seaweed and sea vegetables harvested in the Republic of Ireland.

Violet Hill Studios
www.violethillstudios.com
Centre for healing arts in London. Includes practitioners working with pre and post natal women and babies.

Wholefood Harmony
www.wholefoodharmony.com
Inspires health through delicious, natural cuisine and offers cookery courses, weaning support and food and health coaching.

Printed in Great Britain
by Amazon

21626709R10092